The equilibrium of man's nature, the strength of the body, the capability of receiving external and internal blessings, and the acquisition of worldly and religious advantages, depend ultimately on proper care being shewn for appropriate food. This knowledge distinguishes man from beasts, with whom, as far as mere eating is concerned, he stands upon the same level.

A quotation from Mughal Emperor Akbar's personal records, the *Ain-i-Akbari*, which I feel sums up the Mughal food philosophy.

Dedicated to
my husband and son,
the two boys I love to
beyond the edge of the
ever-expanding
universe.

Saliha Mahmood Ahmed

KHAZANA

HODDER &
STOUGHTON

KHAZANA

Taking a leap into the world of food writing is nothing short of the fulfilment of a lifelong ambition. My first book is a culmination of the countless culinary memories that I have gathered through my life. And thus, through its pages I hope to share a part of myself with you.

In Urdu, the term *khazana* translates as 'treasure trove'. Flicking through the pages of *Khazana*, you will see recipes, artwork and references to the opulent and majestic Mughal Empire. But *Khazana* is not a didactic history book. It is a modern, thoroughly contemporary, twenty-first-century Indo-Persian cookbook that has been inspired by the past, but is made for you to enjoy today and in the future. It does not intend to recreate the ancient Mughal recipes verbatim, but is influenced and inspired by the ancient cookery methods and flavours.

Despite the complexity and extravagance of Mughal design, the recipes in *Khazana* are simple and easy to recreate in even the most basic of kitchens. The beauty of the food is that it does not fall into a specific genre, rather it is a unique amalgamation of the very best of south-east Asia and ancient Persian influences, and even touches upon central Asian cookery.

The recipes are not subtle. My food is bold, proud, full of attitude and deeply steeped in heritage. There are sumptuous recipes to suit every occasion. *Khazana* will be with you at picnics, during festivities and when you entertain guests, whether for brunch, lunch or dinner.

It may sound like a cliché, but I sometimes have to pinch myself when I envisage you picking up *Khazana* from the bookshop shelf, smelling the freshly printed pages and getting lost in the vibrant photography. My heart fills with so much joy when I imagine the pages flung open on a kitchen counter, the pages stained with turmeric, blotches of oil and sticky fingers, knowing that it has inspired, entertained and fulfilled the very purpose for which I intended it to be written.

Saliha
x

Contents

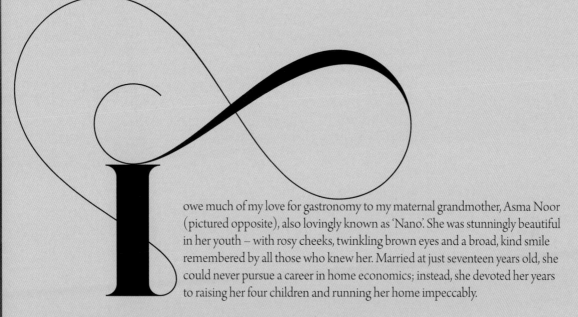

owe much of my love for gastronomy to my maternal grandmother, Asma Noor (pictured opposite), also lovingly known as 'Nano'. She was stunningly beautiful in her youth – with rosy cheeks, twinkling brown eyes and a broad, kind smile remembered by all those who knew her. Married at just seventeen years old, she could never pursue a career in home economics; instead, she devoted her years to raising her four children and running her home impeccably.

Nano was highly innovative. In her kitchen, she invented the most wonderful food for her family together with Shareef the family *khansama* (a male cook in charge of the kitchen). She was never especially extravagant, choosing to live frugally and making use of all that was available to her. Meals were simple, extremely flavoursome and very skilfully prepared. It is this food philosophy of frugality, simplicity and – above all – flavour that has been passed down the generations like a precious gift.

Eating fruit at the end of the meal was mandatory. Nano would sit at the centre of the table peeling mangoes with her chubby fingers. She would hand over the slices of mango to her loved ones, choosing to suck on the stone herself.

My parents are both doctors who moved to England in the eighties after completing their education in Pakistan. Nano visited us in England and would stay for long periods of time, helping with childcare so my parents could purse their careers. She once noticed an apple tree at the back of the NHS accommodation in Sutton-in-Ashfield, Nottinghamshire, where my parents were living. The tree was bursting at the helm with ripe, round, odd-shaped cooking apples that no one wanted. Nano seized the opportunity. For the next month, we ate apples in every form: candied, made into jam, puréed into baby food, pickled, cooked with tamarind in a savoury broth or to add sweetness to lamb curries.

The start of the summer holidays was an extremely exciting time for us all because it would mean the start of an adventure; the ringleader of the adventure was always my dad. A travel enthusiast born with wanderlust, he longed to show his children the world. We travelled through India, Pakistan, Kashmir, the Middle East and central Asia, all the time planning the next meal. Food memories were created at every opportunity, whether eating from roadside stalls (*dhabas*) or fine dining establishments.

It was through our travels that I developed an appreciation of some of the history and architecture of the region. I even remember my mama saying, 'your dad and I studied the Mughal emperors at school in the same way that you studied the Tudors last term'. I would giggle at her amusing commentary, which showed me how very different her early education was from mine. But slowly, with the passage of time, my fascination with the Mughal Empire began. In a way, the Mughals provided a link between my parents' past and our collective present as a family on holiday. They captured my imagination in every way possible. I began to see the Mughal influence everywhere: in architecture, art, Bollywood films, catwalk fashion and contemporary design. I realised that although the Mughal Empire had fallen, their influence lived on.

For many years, cookery remained a serious hobby. I collected mountains of cookery books and magazines and was constantly thinking of my next big project in the kitchen. But, unfortunately, a demanding medical career and motherhood often left me little time for my gastronomic endeavours.

My husband Usman was well aware of my obsessional love of food. It was Usman who in fact applied on my behalf to *MasterChef* 2017. Little to my knowledge, that application form would mark the beginning of the most amazing culinary journey, culminating in me lifting the coveted trophy. I am eternally grateful for the opportunity and all those who made my dreams a reality.

The age of the Mughals (1526–1857)

Most people know very little about the Mughal emperors, except that they were responsible for building one of the Seven Wonders of the World, the magnificent Taj Mahal. The Mughal dynasty actually began in in 1526 when Babur, the ruler of a small principality in central Asia, defeated the Sultan Ibrahim Lodi of Delhi.

Babur was a descendent of two famous central Asian rulers, Timur-i-Leng and Genghis Khan. The dynasty became known as 'Mughal', a corruption of the word 'Mongol'. Initially, Babur did not understand the gastronomy of his newly conquered territories. He dreamt of his long-lost Samarkand, a city in present-day Uzbekistan, with its gurgling streams and lush valleys; 'there is no grapes, quality fruits, mask melons or candles in Hindustan,' he lamented.

At its zenith, the Mughal Empire commanded resources unprecedented in Indian history, covering almost the entirety of the Indian subcontinent. From Gujarat in the west to Bengal in the east, and from present-day Afghanistan to the borders of the Deccan Sultanates, Mughal wealth flourished as the treasures of the defeated kingdoms poured in. Political efficiency along with efficient administration allowed trade to flourish. The Mughals were never too shy to try the new foods from their acquired territories.

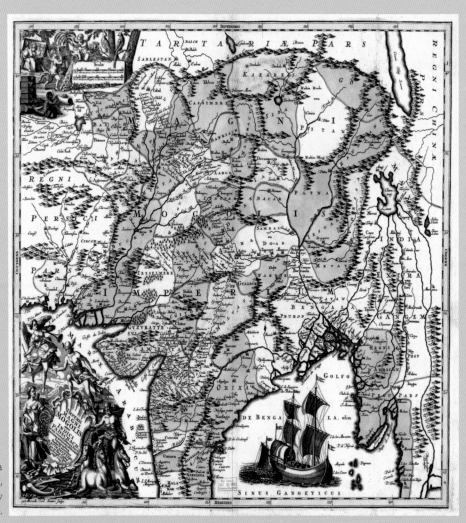

An historical map of India during the Mughal era, circa 1728, coloured by province.

The Mughals regarded Persian culture as the epitome of refinement, even making Farsi their official language. When the Mughal Emperor Humayun was forced into exile, the Shah of Iran gave him refuge; as a gift, Emperor Humayun offered the Shah his Indian cooks. The most wonderful exchange of cultures followed – Emperor Humayun became a great lover of Persian food, partly also because he married a Persian princess. When he returned to India a great number followed him to his royal court: artisans, musicians, painters and – most important of all – Persian cooks.

Food etiquette of the Mughals

Imagine a normal everyday meal in an average Mughal emperor's harem. The emperor would sit cross-legged on white calico placed atop sheets made of leather, known as *dastarkhwan*. Beautiful ladies of the harem would kneel either side of him, serving elaborate meals in gold and silver dishes. Musicians and eunuchs would sing praise for the emperor. At the end of the meal diners would rinse their hands with perfumed water poured from jugs held by servants.

Royal cooks were expected to devise intricate dishes to please and delight their master and impress visiting guests. Food was adorned with gold and silver leaf and huge quantities of nuts. The ethereal perfume of roses wafted from dishes that were laced with premium-quality rose water. Spices were shipped from all parts of the empire: the use of saffron, cardamom, black pepper, cinnamon and cloves was particularly marked. Dishes were often sweet and were subtly warm rather than fiery hot and spicy.

While the average meal was a truly sophisticated and elegant affair, a public banquet was unimaginably opulent. One particularly luxurious feast was held in 1528 by Emperor Babur. He sat beside the *amirs* (generals) of the kingdom, seated in order of their rank. Before the food was served, guests offered Babur presents of rare and precious jewels, fruits, nuts and saffron. The banquet consisted of hundreds of dishes, which guests ate in an octagonal pavilion covered with a special variety of scented grass. And for entertainment, there was an island opposite the pavilion where 'fierce camels and fierce elephants' were fighting.

Food was so important to the Mughals that the imperial kitchen operated as an independent government department with a massive budget of 1,000 rupees a day, enough to procure all manner of exotic foods. The emperors drank water imported from the river Ganges and ice was transported from the hills of Himachal Pradesh, down the Yamuna into the kitchens in Delhi. Interestingly, Mughal menus were finalised in conjunction with the *hakim*, a doctor whose job it was to oversee the nutritional and medicinal properties of food being served.

In the scorching summer heat the Mughal emperors made their way to Kashmir, where they were able to enjoy the temperate climate. It was customary for the imperial kitchen to travel the night before the emperor, to make sure that meals were ready on his arrival. The travelling kitchen consisted of fifty camels, two hundred coolies carrying baskets of crockery, cutlery and cooling utensils atop their heads, and at least fifty milking cows.

It is clear that the Mughals created a lavish, sumptuous and refined food culture, which has undoubtedly left its mark on the gastronomy of the Indian subcontinent today.

There is a wonderful sense of theatre and drama surrounding the Mughals. And with the passage of time the Mughals have captured the imagination of millions in the Indian subcontinent and beyond. Some of the stories have been passed down as word of mouth, making it near impossible to separate fact from fable. But I do not see this as a negative; in some ways, it is this oral history that has kept the Mughals alive over the last few centuries. They are a living entity that had an influence on the past, have an impact on our present and continue to shape the future.

The Taj Mahal at dawn, in Agra, India.

How to use this book

The recipes in this book are suitable for home cooks and won't require any specialist equipment or complicated cooking techniques. However, do take a look at my cook's notes below before you embark on the recipes.

• Before you go out and completely restock your **spice cupboard**, take the time to look through the recipes and decide which ones you want to start with. Build up your spice collection slowly and buy spices in small amounts as they can go stale if left unused for long periods. Store them away from direct sunlight to prolong their shelflife.

• Having said that, if you are **missing a minor ingredient**, do not hesitate to try a recipe anyway; it really won't make too much difference if you don't have the odd ingredient.

• For more **unusual ingredients** and spices, first look in the international aisle of your supermarket. If you cannot find them here, try to locate your local Asian food shop or shop online.

• Never rush the initial stage of cooking your **onions**. This is a vital first step in many Indian recipes and evenly browned, golden onions will add flavour and colour to the completed dish. Cook over a low-medium heat, stirring occasionally, for at least 20 minutes to caramelise them properly.

• Along with the all-important browned onions, **garlic** and **ginger** form the base of many of the recipes in this book. I make up batches of grated garlic cloves and peeled and grated fresh ginger and keep them in my fridge: one garlic clove makes about a teaspoon of grated garlic, while a small thumb-sized piece of ginger will provide about a tablespoon of grated ginger. A Microplane grater is a great little gadget for this but a great time-saving tip is to use shop-bought garlic or ginger paste, available in most supermarkets.

• **Cumin seeds** are used extensively in my recipes – they add a smoky, earthy warmth to dishes, particularly when dry-roasted in a pan. To dry-roast cumin seeds (or any other ingredient that calls for dry-roasting), simply heat them in a small pan without any oil over a medium heat for about 20–30 seconds, or until they release their aroma. Take care as they can burn quickly. You can then either lightly crush or finely grind them in a pestle and mortar.

• Many of my recipes use **Greek yoghurt** and in a handful of cases I have specified to use full-fat Greek yoghurt, by which I mean yoghurt that is 10 per cent fat. In these few instances a higher fat content is essential to prevent the mixture from splitting, or to help achieve a thick, rich texture, so do check the packaging. If full-fat yoghurt is not specified in the recipe, use any Greek yoghurt.

· **Warm water** that is listed in the ingredients is always from a boiled kettle; adding cold water to a pan of ingredients will slow down the cooking process so always keep a full kettle to hand.

· **Tamarind** is a wonderful ingredient that adds a sweet-sour tang to many dishes. To make tamarind pulp, buy a block of pressed tamarind (available from good supermarkets or Asian food stores), break off a chunk and simmer for a couple of minutes in boiling water to soften it, then push through a sieve to extract the pulp. It will keep in an airtight container in the fridge for a month. Don't be tempted to use ready-made tamarind paste or tamarind extract as the texture and flavour are inferior.

· **Kashmiri chilli powder** is used in several of the recipes; it is very mild and has a deep red hue to it. If you have trouble finding it, substitute with a 50:50 mix of chilli powder and hot paprika instead.

· **Salt** is added to taste and in most cases regular table salt is fine, although in a few recipes I have specified sea salt but you can generally use whatever you have.

· Quite a few of my recipes call for **deep-frying** – it's essential for crisp pakoras and samosas! If you don't have a deep fryer you can heat vegetable oil in a deep-sided pan – just don't overcrowd the pan and make sure you let the oil cool fully after use and move to the back of the hob with the handle away from you to avoid any accidents. Don't waste leftover oil – strain the cooled oil through a sieve and store in a jar or plastic bottle until you are ready to use it again.

Conversion tables

Measurements are metric throughout the recipes in this book. If you prefer to use imperial measurements, please see the tables below (figures have been rounded up or down for convenience).

WEIGHT

25g	1 oz
50g	2 oz
100g	3½ oz
150g	5 oz
200g	7 oz
250g	9 oz
300g	10 oz
400g	14 oz
500g	1 lb 2 oz
1 kg	2¼ lb

VOLUME

5ml		1 teaspoon
15ml		1 tablespoon
30ml	1 fl oz	⅛ cup
60ml	2 fl oz	¼ cup
75ml		⅓ cup
120ml	4 fl oz	½ cup
150ml	5 fl oz	⅔ cup
175ml		¾ cup
250ml	8 fl oz	1 cup
1 litre	1 quart	4 cups

LENGTH

1cm	½ inch
2.5cm	1 inch
15cm	6 inches
20cm	8 inches
25cm	10 inches
30cm	12 inches

OVEN TEMPERATURES

°Celsius	°Fahrenheit
140	275
150	300
160	325
180	350
190	375
200	400
220	425
230	450

Recipe suggestions

BREAKFASTS & BRUNCHES

Mughal Spiced Aubergine Kuku (page 46)

Mughal Eggs & Beans (page 175)

Missi Pancakes (page 191)

Watermelon Infused with Hibiscus, Fennel & Cardamom (page 226)

Emperor's Mango Shrikhand Pudding (page 244)

LIGHT LUNCHES

Tadka Carrot Salad with Cumin, Coriander & Mustard Seed Dressing (page 26)

Spinach, Yoghurt & Walnut Soup (page 36)

Roasted Sweet Potato, Chilli, Honey & Tamarind with Toasted Peanuts (page 44)

Masala Livers on Toast with Pickled Ginger, Coriander & Crispy Onions (page 115)

Citrus Semolina Fried Sardines with Preserved Lemon Relish (page 132)

QUICK WEEKDAY DINNERS

Pasand Steak with Cucumber, Coriander & Mint Raita (page 66)

Chicken Thigh & Sour Mango Curry with Coriander Rice (page 96)

Peshawar-style Turkey Chapli Kebab with Burnt Tomatoes & Buttery Rice (page 112)

Sea Bass, Chilli & Saffron Butter Baked in Lavash (page 140)

Mughal Baked Cod Korma (page 143)

PICNICS

Crunchy Potato & Kidney Bean Tikki Bites with Summer Green Relish (page 48)

Nargisi Kofta Scotch Eggs (page 50)

Cumin, Turmeric & Ajwain Nimki Straws (page 54)

Almond & Smoked Fish Koftas with Watercress & Toasted Almond Salad (page 138)

Afghani Potato & Spinach Bolani (page 194)

Coconut Rose Ladoos (page 254)

BARBECUE/TANDOORI DISHES

Lamb & Potato Seekh Kebabs (page 90)

Smoked Chicken & Basil Kebabs with Beetroot Basil Salad & Beetroot Buttermilk Raita (page 98)

Malai Chicken Bites (page 111)

Fiery King Prawns with Spiced Yoghurt Dipping Sauce (page 146)

VEGETARIAN FEAST

Whole Roast Cauliflower with Saffron, Cashews, Coconut & Chilli (page 158)

Saag & Cornmeal Bread (page 162)

Sour & Spicy Pink Radishes (page 164)

Creamy Mung Dal with Cumin Butter & Sourdough Toast (page 169)

Cashew Dum Biryani with Potato & White Poppy Seeds (page 190)

Radish & Mung Bean Parathas (page 192)

EASY ENTERTAINING

Kale Pakoras with Charred Tomato & Tamarind Broth (page 40)

Mughal Spiced Nut Mix (page 57)

Onion & Saffron Roast Chicken Drumsticks with Sweet Cucumber Salad (page 105)

Honey & Cardamom Quails with Spiced Figs & Bulgur Wheat (page 120)

Sticky Tamarind & Orange Salmon (page 134)

Turkish Delight Pots with Dark Chocolate & Rose Cream (page 242)

SPRING/SUMMER

Guava, Peach, Black Salt & Mint (page 32)
Anaarkali Pomegranate Shorba (page 34)
Courgettes Stuffed with Chana Dal & Tamarind (page 152)
Watermelon Curry (page 168)
Crème Fraîche & Rose Ice Cream
with Honey-glazed Figs (page 234)

———————————— • ————————————

AUTUMN

Lamb Braised with Prunes & Rose Water (page 79)
Roughan Josh with Saffron Mash &
Pickled Red Onion Salad (page 84)
Stewed Poussin with Saffron & Butter Beans (page 114)
Mountain Mushrooms (page 174)
Chickpea & Lamb Chop Polow (page 184)

———————————— • ————————————

WINTER

Jerusalem Artichoke Chaat with Tamarind
& Sweetened Curd (page 42)
Lamb Shanks in Pomegranate & Date Syrup with Aubergine
& Chickpea Couscous (page 70)
Steamed Lamb Manty with Tomato & Garlic Sauce (page 82)
Roast Kashmiri Duck with Spiced Plums & Caramelised Walnuts (page 118)
Beetroot Curry with Mint & Sour Cream (page 160)
Blackberry & Star Anise Chutney (page 205)

DIPPING PLATTERS
(WITH FLATBREADS, VEGETABLES, POPPADUMS)

Mango, Strawberry & Tamarind Chutney (page 206)

Whipped Walnut Relish (page 208)

Coriander, Cashew & Golden Sultana Dip (page 213)

Pumpkin, Honey & Saffron Raita (page 215)

Turmeric Aubergine & Tadka Yoghurt Raita (page 216)

———————— • ————————

BEST OF BRITISH, MUGHAL STYLE

Lamb, Mint & Peas (page 78)

Sea Bream Pakoras with Brown Sauce & Spicy Chips (page 130)

'Patta Gobi' Spiced Cabbage (page 172)

Eastern Cauliflower Piccalilli (page 214)

Smoky Eastern Ketchup (page 220)

Shahi Tukre (page 239)

———————— • ————————

AN EXTRAVAGANT MUGHAL FEAST

Leg of Lamb Braised in Yoghurt with Turmeric Roast Potatoes (page 80)

Rose-scented Chicken & Rose Shorba with Saffron Rice (page 102)

Emperor's Venison Shami Kebabs with Mint & Tomato Salad (page 124)

Smoky Spiced Aubergine & Pomegranate Vol-au-vents (page 154)

Jewelled Persian Rice (page 180)

Sour Cherry, Pistachio & Sesame Naan (page 198)

Kashmiri Plum & Almond Chutney (page 204)

Saffron-poached Apple Murabba (page 230)

Sandalwood Ice Cream (page 238)

Betel Leaf Mouth Freshener (page 258)

Salads, Soups & Starters

The Mughal emperors were the embodiment of an oxymoron if there ever was one. While on the one hand they were fearless warriors conquering Hindustan, on the other they were tender, passionate lovers capable of building the Taj Mahal for lost love.

In the spirit of the Mughals, their food is also full of contrasts. For example, despite dishes being enriched with clarified butter, saffron, nuts and dried fruit, they are still imbued with the subtle flavours of cardamom, rose, fennel and citrusy herbs. While there is no doubt that the food was extravagant and unashamedly celebratory, due diligence was also given to the medicinal and digestive properties of ingredients.

For such a varied food culture, the Mughals did not eat salads in the same way that we do today. Raw vegetables were usually eaten mixed with yoghurt in the form of a raita. Perhaps the warm weather was not conducive to growing delicate leaves and made food perish easily. Nonetheless, in the spirit of invention, I have created some modern Indo-Persian-style salads inspired by elements of Mughal cuisine and I am certain they would have pleased even the emperors themselves.

Although the Mughals did not eat street food per se, nowadays you can almost always guarantee an array of fantastic food stalls outside Mughal tourist hotspots. Like the thousands of visitors, I am also lucky to have formed many culinary memories through the street food I have eaten while admiring the Mughal architectural masterpieces of south-east Asia. Here I have used ancient Mughal flavours and cookery methods to develop modern-day Indian street food recipes.

with Cumin, Coriandar & Mustard Seed Dressing
Tadka Carrot Salad

SERVES 2–4

500g carrots, peeled and grated

75ml vegetable oil

1 teaspoon brown mustard seeds

1 heaped tablespoon cumin seeds

½ teaspoon ground turmeric

1 teaspoon chilli flakes

½ bunch of fresh coriander, leaves and stalks finely chopped

Juice of 1 large lemon

3 tablespoons honey

Salt, to taste

The fondest of childhood memories come from watching my mother cook. She would apply a *tadka* to her lentils; a traditional Mughal technique where spices were tempered in hot oil, transforming into a deeper, earthier version of themselves.

In contrast to my mother, I like to 'tadka' raw vegetables – these carrots make a fantastic light lunch or accompaniment to any meat feast. The perfume of spices sizzling in hot oil is completely intoxicating.

———————————

Squeeze out any excess moisture from the grated carrot and put it into a large bowl.

Heat the oil in a pan over a medium heat until it is very hot but not quite at smoking point. First add the mustard seeds and cumin seeds to the hot oil – they should start sizzling and popping immediately – then add the turmeric and chilli flakes, stirring quickly to prevent the spices from burning. Carefully pour the hot oil onto the grated carrots. Stand back from the pan, as the spices may pop.

Add the chopped coriander to the carrots along with lemon juice, honey and plenty of salt. Stir all the ingredients well and serve the salad at room temperature.

 NB *Instead of carrots you could also use grated beetroot, thinly sliced cauliflower, shredded red cabbage or even shaved fennel.*

Honey-roasted Grapes,
Labneh, Roasted Walnuts
& Persian Herbs

200g purple or red grapes
(e.g. Muscat)

2 tablespoons honey

½ teaspoon chilli flakes

1 teaspoon vegetable oil

60g walnuts, roughly chopped

1 tablespoon tamarind pulp

4 tablespoons extra virgin olive oil

Handful of rocket leaves

Handful of fresh tarragon

Handful of fresh flat-leaf
parsley leaves

6–8 radishes, quartered

200g labneh (see Note)

Handful of pomegranate seeds

Sea salt, to taste

Interestingly, the Mughals were not well known for serving elaborate or inventive summery salads at their tables. In contrast, Persian meals often begin with a platter of sabzi khordan, a selection of fresh herbs, walnuts and feta served in generous handfuls.

The Mughal emperors were, of course, heavily influenced by Persian culture and borrowed many Persian traits and customs as well as their recipes. This salad uses some of the ingredients found in sabzi khordan and serves them in a new and unexpected way. There is something deeply satisfying about the soft blandness of labneh against sweet grapes and crunchy bitter walnuts – a match made in heaven.

Mix the grapes with the honey, chilli flakes and a tiny pinch of salt in a small pan. Place over a low heat just until they have warmed through and have a sticky outer glaze but still hold their shape. Keep the sticky grapes to one side.

Heat the vegetable oil in a small frying pan and add the chopped walnuts and a little salt. Toast over a low heat until they have browned all over – be careful to not let them burn.

Make a dressing by whisking together the tamarind pulp and olive oil with a pinch of salt. Toss the rocket leaves, tarragon, parsley and radishes in the salad dressing.

Rub a few drops of oil onto your hands and shape the labneh into small balls; if your labneh is too soft to shape, don't worry! You can just as easily use a teaspoon to place small rounds onto the finished salad platter.

To assemble the salad, place the labneh balls, honey-glazed grapes and toasted walnuts over the dressed leaves and radishes. Garnish with a handful of pomegranate seeds before serving.

 NB *To make labneh from scratch, hang 500g full-fat Greek yoghurt in a muslin cloth or clean J-cloth suspended over a bowl for 24 hours in the fridge. The consistency should be that of soft cheese which can be shaped into small bite-sized balls.*

Mint, Roasted Fennel & Pomegranate Salad

SERVES 2–4

2 large fennel bulbs, trimmed at the base

2 tablespoons olive oil, plus extra for brushing

1½ teaspoons fennel seeds, lightly crushed

1 teaspoon chilli flakes

Juice of ½ lemon

Large handful of pomegranate seeds

1 tablespoon pomegranate molasses

100g rocket leaves

Bunch of fresh mint, leaves picked

Salt, to taste

The Mughals felt that it was extremely important to understand the medicinal property of food. Mint and fennel seeds were thought to ease digestion – particularly when rich, fatty meat dishes were on the menu. This salad is light and summery and would be the perfect accompaniment to any roast meat. I will, of course, let you judge its digestive properties for yourself…

Preheat the oven to 200°C (180°C fan), gas mark 6.

Holding the fennel bulbs upright, cut them into approximately 1cm-thick slices vertically from top to bottom. Brush both sides of each fennel slice with olive oil and arrange on a baking sheet. Sprinkle over the crushed fennel seeds, chilli flakes and some salt and put into the oven for about 15 minutes, or until the fennel has softened and charred slightly. Set aside to cool.

Meanwhile, whisk together the lemon juice, olive oil, pomegranate seeds and pomegranate molasses to make a fruity dressing.

When you are ready to serve, dress the rocket leaves and fennel slices with the dressing and arrange on a large platter. Scatter the mint leaves over the salad and enjoy the fruity, aniseed taste sensation immediately.

Guava, Peach, Black Salt & Mint

SERVES 4

3 ripe guavas

3 ripe peaches

Handful of fresh mint leaves

½ teaspoon black salt (or use Himalayan pink salt or sea salt)

½ teaspoon amchoor (mango powder)

½ teaspoon cumin seeds, dry-roasted and ground

1 heaped teaspoon caster sugar

3 tablespoons fresh orange juice

As a child, I was able to accompany my grandmother on her numerous social engagements. She would meet her very large and extended family for laid-back lunch dates, committee meetings and kitty parties; these were a popular way for women to socialise by being part of an informal savings club and were held once a month in the afternoons. Any excuse to chitchat over nibbles… I did not understand much of the family gossip but was certainly entertained by the food being served. When peaches and guavas were in season this dish often found its way to the table. If you can't get hold of guavas, any other sweet tropical fruit like papaya, mango or even fresh apricots would serve as a worthy substitute.

Using a sharp knife, cut the guavas into thin slices and place in a bowl. Halve and stone the peaches and then cut each half into thin slices; add to the guavas in the bowl.

Slice the mint leaves into thin strips – you may find it easier to roll a few leaves into a tight bundle and then slice them crossways. Add the mint to the fruit along with the black salt, amchoor and cumin seeds. Stir in the sugar and orange juice and allow to rest for at least half an hour before serving.

Anaarkali Pomegranate Shorba

SERVES 4

400g pomegranate seeds, plus a handful to garnish

400ml chicken stock

100g butter

2 onions, very thinly sliced

1 teaspoon grated ginger

1 teaspoon cumin seeds, dry-roasted and ground

1 teaspoon chilli flakes

180g coarsely chopped baby spinach, plus extra to garnish

1 x 400g tin chickpeas, rinsed and drained

Salt, to taste

The Mughal emperors had a great love affair with the pomegranate. Legend dictates that Emperor Akbar's most adored concubine was called Anaarkali, which means 'pomegranate blossom'. According to some sources, Anaarkali's sad demise followed her tempestuous affair with Emperor Akbar's son! Controversial…

This shorba is a delightful savoury pomegranate soup. Similar soups are enjoyed today in parts of central Asia, an area that has, of course, seen the presence of the Mughals.

Start by blitzing the pomegranate seeds and chicken stock in a food processor or blender. Pass this mixture through a sieve and then put to one side; discard the seeds.

Melt the butter in a large pan over a low heat and add the onions. Sweat the onions gently for about 15 minutes; when they start turning a light golden colour, add the ginger, cumin seeds and chilli flakes. Stir well to release all the flavour from the spices and to stop them catching.

Now add the spinach and chickpeas to the onions and spices and stir well. The spinach will wilt down quite quickly and release some moisture into the pan. Take a potato masher and smash some of the chickpeas in the pan to break them down slightly – the idea is that the chickpeas are not left whole.

Now pour in the pomegranate/chicken stock and give the mixture a good stir. Bring the shorba to the boil and simmer for about 5 minutes, then season with salt. Serve garnished with a few extra chopped spinach leaves and pomegranate seeds.

Spinach, Yoghurt & Walnut Soup

SERVES 4

50g butter

2 onions, thinly sliced

50g walnuts, blitzed in a food processor

1 tablespoon plain flour

500ml chicken stock

Pinch of saffron threads, soaked in a few tablespoons of warm water

1 teaspoon dried mint

1 teaspoon dried fenugreek leaves

½ teaspoon chilli flakes

300g baby spinach leaves

300g full-fat Greek yoghurt

Salt, to taste

NB *If you find the soup is too thick, feel free to add a small amount of warm water to adjust it to your preferred consistency.*

When I was researching the ancient Mughal manuscripts for this book, I stumbled across a recipe for a soup called eshkinah shirazi. I adapted the historical recipe and made it for my husband who is not usually a fan of soup. To my delight, he absolutely adored its warming, nutty autumnal tone.

On browsing through my collection of Persian cookery books, I found a distinctly different recipe for an Iranian soup, but with the same name, eshkinah shirazi. It's fascinating to think how these recipes have evolved so differently over time.

Melt the butter in a large pan over a low heat. Add the onions and cook gently until the onions are caramelised and have turned a rich golden brown – this can take up to half an hour. Add the ground walnuts to the caramelised onions followed by the plain flour and allow the mixture to brown, stirring constantly to prevent the mixture from burning. Pour in the chicken stock slowly, stirring to prevent lumps from forming. The soup should thicken at this stage.

Stir the saffron and its soaking liquid, dried mint, dried fenugreek leaves and chilli flakes into the soup and allow to simmer over a low heat for 5–10 minutes.

Meanwhile, put the spinach and yoghurt into a food processor or blender and blend until completely smooth. Turn the heat of the pan down to the lowest setting and then whisk in the spinach and yoghurt mixture, a tablespoon at a time, until well combined. Keep the heat as low as possible, otherwise the yoghurt may split and curdle. Season with plenty of salt and serve immediately.

Kale Pakoras

with Charred Tomato & Tamarind Broth

SERVES 4

For the Pakoras

75g gram flour

1 heaped tablespoon cornflour

½ teaspoon bicarbonate of soda

1 teaspoon chilli powder

1 teaspoon cumin seeds, coarsely ground

1 teaspoon coriander seeds, coarsely ground

½ teaspoon salt

100g kale leaves, tough stems removed

Vegetable oil, for deep-frying

For the Broth

750g cherry tomatoes

2 garlic cloves, peeled but left whole

1 green chilli (medium strength)

Olive oil, for brushing

½ teaspoon grated ginger

2 tablespoons tamarind pulp

½ teaspoon ground cumin

200ml warm water (optional)

Pinch of sugar (optional)

Salt, to taste

I remember eating pakoras with smoky tomato chutney from a roadside stall outside the Red Fort in Delhi, a fine example of Mughal architecture. The memory is so profound, that I am transported back to that very moment every time I catch a whiff of gram flour being deep-fried. Kale is a wonderful, slightly bitter green vegetable and takes extremely well to being battered and fried, becoming feather light, airy and crisp. It tastes delicious with this smoky tomato broth – a fantastic dish to warm you up on a rainy day.

First make the broth. Halve the cherry tomatoes and arrange skin-side up on baking sheet, together with the garlic cloves and chilli. Brush with olive oil and place under a hot grill until the skins char. Tip into a food processor or blender with the grated ginger and blitz to a smooth purée. Transfer the purée to a pan and add the tamarind pulp and ground cumin. Simmer for 10–15 minutes over a low heat, allowing all the flavours to amalgamate with one another. The broth will be quite thick but if you like it thinner (like my mum) you can stir in the measured hot water at this stage. Taste and season with salt and a touch of sugar if the tomatoes are too acidic.

Meanwhile, mix the gram flour, cornflour, bicarbonate of soda, chilli powder, ground cumin and coriander seeds and salt to the flour. Whisk in just enough warm water to form a batter that has the consistency of double cream. Mix the kale into the batter and stir to coat well.

Heat the vegetable oil in a large pan or deep fryer until a drop of batter sizzles in the oil. Deep-fry the kale leaves in small batches until they turn crisp and the batter takes on a deep golden colour. Remove and drain on kitchen paper while you make the next batch.

Serve the crisp kale pakoras with the smoky tomato broth.

with Tamarind & Sweetened Curd
Jerusalem Artichoke Chaat

For the Jerusalem Artichoke

450 grams Jerusalem artichoke

1 egg

½ teaspoon red chilli powder

4 tablespoons fine semolina

1 teaspoon chaat masala

For the Green Chutney

½ bunch of fresh coriander

½ bunch of fresh mint leaves
(removed from the stalks)

1 green chilli

Juice of ½ lemon

1 tablespoon Greek yoghurt

Salt

For the Sweetened Curd

250ml Greek yoghurt

2 tablespoons honey

½ teaspoon salt

Garnishes

3 tablespoons ready-made
tamarind chutney

Handful of chopped fresh
coriander

Handful of pomegranate seeds

Chaat masala is a wonderful salty, slightly sulphurous, tart spice mix. I often buy it ready-made – look in Asian food stores or large supermarkets. It is used to make a dish called chaat, a ridiculously moreish south-east Asian street food dish.

The origin of chaat masala is hotly debated. Some food historians claim that it was first made in Muradabad, a small brass-making region in Rajasthan, India. Descendants of the Mughal emperors founded Muradabad, and are rumoured to have enjoyed this savoury spice mix.

Bring a large pan of water to the boil, add the artichokes and boil for 8 minutes, then drain in a colander and allow them to dry off. When they are cool enough to handle, cut the artichokes into approximately 1cm-thick slices (no need to remove the skin).

Prepare the green chutney by putting the coriander, mint leaves, chilli, lemon juice, yoghurt and a pinch of salt into a small food processor or blender. Blitz to form a smooth-textured sauce – add a few tablespoons of water if the mixture is not blending easily. Taste and add more salt if you think it needs it.

To make the sweetened curd, whisk the yoghurt lightly with the honey and salt.

Lightly beat the egg in a shallow bowl and whisk in the chilli powder and a pinch of salt. Put the semolina in a separate bowl. Dip the artichoke slices first in the egg and then in the semolina, making sure each slice is coated evenly with egg and semolina.

Heat the oil in a large pan or deep fryer until a pinch of semolina sizzles in the hot oil. Deep-fry the artichokes in small batches over a medium-low heat until they are golden brown and crisp on the outside and soft in the centre, about 3–5 minutes. Drain on kitchen paper and sprinkle over the chaat masala.

To serve, arrange the deep-fried Jerusalem artichoke slices in a serving dish and drizzle over the green chutney, sweetened curd and tamarind chutney. Scatter with chopped fresh coriander and pomegranate seeds and serve immediately.

Roasted Sweet Potato,
Chilli, Honey & Tamarind
with Toasted Peanuts

SERVES 2–4

4 large sweet potatoes, scrubbed

Olive oil

½ red onion, thinly sliced

1 tomato, diced

2 tablespoons tamarind pulp

Juice of ½ lemon

1 teaspoon chaat masala

1 tablespoon honey or maple syrup

1 teaspoon chilli flakes

Handful of toasted salted peanuts, roughly chopped

Handful of chopped fresh coriander

Salt, to taste

I first tried roasted sweet potatoes outside the famous Baadshahi Mosque in old Lahore, a beautiful Mughal monument. The sweet potatoes were roasted whole in warm ash and the soft flesh was topped with fresh lime juice, a concoction of fiery spices and tamarind pulp. The harmonious combination of sweet, salty and sour flavours really was lip-smackingly good.

—————————————

Preheat the oven to 200°C (180°C fan), gas mark 6.

Leaving the skins on, cut the sweet potatoes into thick chunks or wedges, then tip into a baking tray, drizzle with olive oil and season with salt. Roast for about 30 minutes, or until the sweet potatoes are cooked through and slightly brown and caramelised at the edges.

Transfer the roasted sweet potatoes to a bowl and stir in the red onion, tomato, tamarind pulp, lemon juice, chaat masala, honey or maple syrup, chilli flakes and a tablespoon of olive oil until everything is combined.

Tip into a serving dish, then scatter over the chopped toasted peanuts and coriander. Serve immediately.

Mughal Spiced Aubergine Kuku

SERVES 4

2 medium aubergines
Olive oil
200g leeks, thinly sliced
1 garlic clove, finely grated
½ teaspoon ground turmeric
6 eggs
25g chopped fresh coriander
Pinch of saffron threads, soaked in
a few tablespoons of warm water
1 teaspoon chilli flakes
2 tablespoons full-fat Greek
yoghurt
½ teaspoon baking powder
1 large potato, peeled, boiled and
thickly sliced
Salt, to taste

Many ancient Mughal cookery books document recipes for kuku bademjan, or aubergine frittata. Today, kuku is enjoyed extensively in Iran rather than the Indian subcontinent, where it is made without using much in the way of spices.

My Mughal-inspired aubergine frittata can be enjoyed piping hot from the oven, at room temperature or cold the next day in a lunchbox – it's fantastic to take to a picnic. I use leeks for flavour and colour, but you could also use caramelised shallots and the final results would be sublime.

_____

Preheat the oven to 200°C (180°C fan), gas mark 6.

Slice the aubergines into 1cm-thick rounds, brush them with olive oil on both sides and place on a baking sheet. Transfer to the oven for 20 minutes until the aubergines have softened and cooked through. Set aside to cool.

Add a drizzle of olive oil to a frying pan and place over a medium heat. Add the leeks, garlic and turmeric and cook, stirring, until the leeks have softened, about 5 minutes. Remove from the heat.

Crack the eggs into a bowl and whisk lightly. Add the coriander, saffron and its soaking liquid, chilli flakes, yoghurt, baking powder and salt. Whisk all the ingredients together then gently add the cooled aubergine slices, leeks and boiled potato to the egg mixture.

Pour the frittata mixture into a medium ovenproof non-stick pan (which you may wish to line with greaseproof paper) and transfer to the oven. Bake for 30 minutes, or until the frittata is set and the surface is golden. Serve hot or cold, cut into wedges.

Crunchy Potato & Kidney Bean Tikki Bites

with Summer Green Relish

SERVES 4

For the Tikki Bites

450g mashed Maris Piper potatoes

1 x 400g tin red kidney beans, rinsed and drained

2 teaspoons anardana (pomegranate powder)

1 teaspoon cumin seeds, dry-roasted and coarsely ground

4 tablespoons finely chopped fresh coriander

1 red chilli, finely diced

1 tablespoon melted butter

1 egg yolk

75g plain flour

1 beaten egg

100g breadcrumbs

Vegetable oil, for deep-frying

Salt, to taste

For the Relish

2 ripe tomatoes, finely chopped

½ green chilli, finely chopped

½ bunch of fresh coriander, finely chopped

Juice ½ lemon

1 teaspoon caster sugar

Salt, to taste

Tikki, bite-sized potato croquettes, are eaten throughout north India and Pakistan. They really are incredibly moreish. The addition of kidney beans gives these little morsels of delight an added textural dimension as well as giving an amazing pale pink hue to the croquette mix. They are totally wonderful served as a canapé or light starter.

Put the mashed potato, drained kidney beans, anardana, cumin seeds, chopped coriander, chilli, melted butter and egg yolk into a large bowl. Add salt to taste and then mash the mixture with a fork until the spices are well combined and some of the kidney beans have broken up. Transfer the mixture to the fridge and allow to rest for 1 hour.

Rub a little oil onto your hands. Take walnut-sized portions of the mixture and then roll them into small rounds. Place on a greased plate or tray and chill for a further 15–20 minutes (this will make them much easier to crumb). Meanwhile, make the relish. Add all the relish ingredients to a bowl and stir well to combine.

Put the flour, beaten egg and breadcrumbs into separate bowls. Roll the tikki bites in the flour, followed by the egg and then the breadcrumbs until all the bites are coated.

Heat the vegetable oil in a large pan or deep fryer until a pinch of breadcrumbs sizzles in the hot oil. Deep-fry the tikki bites in batches until they are golden brown, about 3 minutes. Remove from the pan with a slotted spoon and drain on kitchen paper while you cook the next batch.

Serve the tikkis while they are still warm with the green relish on the side.

Nargisi Kofta Scotch Eggs

500g minced chicken

3 beaten eggs

4 tablespoons finely chopped fresh coriander

1 heaped teaspoon chilli flakes

2 heaped teaspoons anardana (pomegranate powder)

2 teaspoons cumin seeds, dry-roasted

1 teaspoon gram flour

6 eggs

Plain flour, for dusting

250g breadcrumbs (fresh or panko)

Vegetable oil, for deep-frying

Nargisi kofta is spiced meat encasing an egg, traditionally slow-cooked in a very rich tomato-based sauce. *Nargisi* refers to the narcissus flower – the idea being that that the kofta meat encasing the egg resembles the narcissus flower when cut into quarters. I use Mughal-style seasonings to make a spiced and fragrant chicken kofta. My version is more like a scotch egg than a curry and is wonderful for a lunchbox or picnic.

Put the minced chicken, one of the beaten eggs, the coriander, chilli flakes, anardana, cumin seeds and gram flour into a large bowl and mix until combined. Put the mixture into the fridge to chill.

Bring a pan of water to the boil and carefully add the eggs. Boil for 5–6 minutes, then immediately take the eggs off the heat and place them in a bowl of cool water. Shell the eggs carefully under the water (if you find that the egg white has not yet set, boil the remaining eggs for a further 90 seconds, and then re-attempt shelling under water). Once peeled, roll the eggs in the plain flour and set aside.

Divide the chilled chicken mixture into six equal portions. Roll each portion into a ball and transfer onto six individual pieces of cling film. Flatten a ball with the palm of your hand to form a thin patty. Wrap the patty around a floured egg, smoothing out the join and making sure that no part of the egg is visible. Use the cling film to help you spread the patty evenly over the egg. Repeat the steps for all six eggs and transfer to the fridge to chill.

Remove the cling film from the koftas and roll them in more flour, making sure that no area of raw meat is left uncovered. Put the remaining beaten eggs and breadcrumbs into separate bowls. Dip each kofta into the beaten egg, ensuring the egg touches every surface of the floured kofta. Finally, coat with breadcrumbs.

Heat vegetable oil for deep-frying in a large pan or deep fryer until a pinch of breadcrumbs sizzles in the hot oil. Deep-fry the scotch eggs in batches of two or three over a medium heat for about 5 minutes, or until the crumb is golden brown. Remove with a slotted spoon and drain on kitchen paper.

Serve hot or cold, and for perfection, with a dollop of tomato ketchup and my Eastern Cauliflower Piccalilli (see page 214).

Illustrated overleaf (from left to right):

Summer Green Relish; Nargisi Kofta Scotch Eggs; Eastern Cauliflower Piccalilli; Watermelon Infused with Hibiscus, Fennel & Cardamom; Afghani Potato & Spinach Bolani; Crunchy Potato & Kidney Bean Tikki Bites; and Coconut Rose Ladoos.

Cumin, Turmeric & Ajwain Nimki Straws

SERVES 4–6

50g butter
1 teaspoon ground turmeric
2 teaspoons cumin seeds
1 teaspoon ajwain (carom) seeds
1 sheet of ready-rolled puff pastry
1 beaten egg
Sea salt, to taste

Given the fact that I am a serial grazer and need snacks to keep me going through the day, I could not have written this book without including this recipe. Nimki is a snack originating from the Mughal era, which is still eaten today in India and Pakistan. It is essentially pastry that is seasoned with cumin, ajwain seeds and turmeric and then deep-fried in ghee, but my version uses puff pastry and the oven for a result that is light, crisp and ever so moreish. All you need with these straws is an accompanying cup of strong tea, although it really should be chai...

———————————————

Melt the butter in a small pan and mix in the turmeric, cumin and ajwain seeds. Allow the butter to cool slightly.

Unroll the puff pastry sheet on your worktop, but do not take it off the greaseproof paper it came in. Generously brush the butter over the puff pastry sheet, sprinkle with sea salt and transfer to the fridge for 30 minutes. Meanwhile, line two baking sheets with baking parchment.

Use a sharp knife to cut the pastry into 12 strips of equal width and lay them on the lined sheets, twisting the pastry from either end to create the straw effect and spacing them about 3cm apart. Put the trays of prepared straws in the freezer for 30 minutes.

Preheat the oven to 200°C (180°C fan), gas mark 6. Brush the straws lightly with beaten egg and bake them from frozen for 15–18 minutes, or until golden brown and crisp.

Mughal Spiced Nut Mix

SERVES 4-6

150g raw cashew nuts

100g untoasted almonds

100g untoasted walnuts

100g shelled untoasted peanuts

50g char maghaz (raw white melon seeds)

1 teaspoon cumin seeds

2 tablespoons blossom honey

3 tablespoons vegetable oil

1 heaped teaspoon sea salt

½ teaspoon garam masala

1 heaped teaspoon cayenne pepper

1 tablespoon demerara sugar

100g golden sultanas

50g sour cherries

A wonderful way of using nuts, incredibly moreish and fantastic to munch on before a meal to whet the appetite. You will be surprised at how fast they disappear so don't hesitate to make them in bigger batches. They will store well in a jar for around a week.

Preheat the oven to 190°C (170°C fan), gas mark 5 and line a baking sheet with baking parchment.

Mix all the nuts and the melon seeds in a bowl together with the cumin seeds, honey, vegetable oil and sea salt. Stir well to ensure that each nut is coated well.

Tip the nuts onto the lined baking sheet and spread out in a single layer. Roast for about 15 minutes until the nuts are beautifully brown and caramelised but not burnt. Stir the nuts every 4–5 minutes while they are still in the oven to ensure that they toast evenly.

When the nuts come out of the oven dust them evenly with the garam masala, cayenne pepper and demerara sugar and mix in the sultanas and sour cherries. Stir the nuts gently on the baking sheet from time to time as they are cooling.

Once the nuts have cooled completely, transfer to a clean airtight jar to keep the nuts crisp.

Pista Samosa

SERVES 4

For the Filling

2 teaspoons light olive oil

½ red onion, finely chopped

2 garlic cloves, finely grated

1 teaspoon grated ginger

½ teaspoon garam masala

1 green chilli, finely chopped

¼ teaspoon grated nutmeg

150g minced lamb

80g shelled pistachios, roughly chopped

1 teaspoon rose water

Good pinch of saffron threads, soaked in a few tablespoons of warm water

1 tablespoon chopped fresh mint leaves

1 tablespoon chopped fresh coriander

Salt, to taste

For the Pastry

150g plain flour

1 teaspoon salt

2 tablespoons light olive oil

Vegetable oil, for frying

Today the samosa is considered a quintessentially Indian delicacy. In actual fact, the history of the samosa is far more complex and cosmopolitan. Food historians agree that the Mughals helped popularise this dish on the Indian subcontinent, but its origins seem to lie in the Middle East and central Asia, where it was enjoyed centuries earlier. In this recipe I use pistachios (*pista*) to create the most wonderful nutty mince stuffing.

First make the filling. Pour the oil into a large frying pan and fry the red onion over a low-medium heat for about 5 minutes until softened and golden brown. Stir through the garlic, ginger, garam masala, green chilli and nutmeg, then increase the heat slightly and add the minced lamb to the pan. Fry off the mince until it is cooked through and most of the moisture has been absorbed. You may need to mash the mince against the side of the pan with your spoon to ensure that any lumps of mince break down.

Remove the cooked lamb mixture from the heat and allow it to cool. Add the pistachios, rose water, saffron and its soaking liquid, mint and coriander. Stir well to combine and season to taste with salt. The filling is now ready to use.

To prepare the pastry, put the flour, salt and oil into a large bowl. Adding just enough water to form a firm dough, use your hands to bring the dough together. Knead gently until the dough no longer sticks to the bowl and then divide the dough into small balls that are about the size of a lime. Cover the dough balls with a piece of cling film to prevent them from drying out.

Roll each dough ball out on a lightly floured surface into a circle that is less than a millimetre thick and has a diameter of about 15cm. Cut the circle in half to make two semicircles. Brush a little water along the straight edge of one semicircle and pick it up. Form into a cone shape by folding the two corners in so that they meet in the middle and one wet edge overlaps the other. Press the dough edges together to seal.

Fill the dough cone with the filling to about three-quarters of the way up. Brush the remaining flap of pastry with a little more water and seal by pinching the edge together with your fingers, or crimp using a fork. Continue with all the pastry and filling (you should have about 12 samosas). Place the prepared samosas on a greased tray and cover with a damp cloth or piece of cling film so they don't dry out. (You can make these up to a day ahead and chill in the fridge or freeze for another day; simply defrost for about 1 hour before frying.)

When you are ready to serve the samosas, heat the vegetable oil in a large pan or deep fryer; it's hot enough when a small piece of pastry dropped in sizzles immediately. Deep-fry the samosas in small batches for about 30 seconds on each side (turn them carefully with a slotted spoon), or until they are golden brown and crisp. Remove from the oil and drain on kitchen paper. Serve hot with any pickle or relish of your choice.

Meat

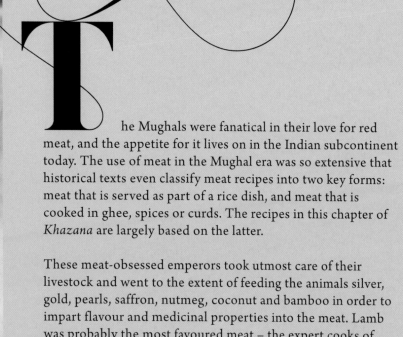

The Mughals were fanatical in their love for red meat, and the appetite for it lives on in the Indian subcontinent today. The use of meat in the Mughal era was so extensive that historical texts even classify meat recipes into two key forms: meat that is served as part of a rice dish, and meat that is cooked in ghee, spices or curds. The recipes in this chapter of *Khazana* are largely based on the latter.

These meat-obsessed emperors took utmost care of their livestock and went to the extent of feeding the animals silver, gold, pearls, saffron, nutmeg, coconut and bamboo in order to impart flavour and medicinal properties into the meat. Lamb was probably the most favoured meat – the expert cooks of the imperial kitchens felt that it was lighter and much more easily digested than beef (the Emperor Humayan is known to have found beef tasteless and tough in comparison to lamb). And although beef was not prohibited by the Mughals, many officials of the Mughal court would have been of the Hindu, rather than Muslim faith, making beef strictly prohibited from a religious standpoint.

The meat-based dishes of the Mughal era were undoubtedly sophisticated beyond their time. Great care was taken to ensure that the meat that had been reared with such love and attention was also cooked to perfection and tenderised fully. The term *galawat* referred to the use of softening agents such as raw papaya, lemon juice, vinegar or curds. These same techniques are still used extensively by Indian chefs aspiring to serve meat that is so tender and moist that it practically falls off the bone.

Pasand Steak
with Cucumber, Coriander & Mint Raita

SERVES 4

For the Steak

1 teaspoon ground cumin

1 teaspoon ground coriander

1 large garlic clove, finely grated

1 heaped teaspoon grated ginger

1 heaped teaspoon hot paprika

1 teaspoon chilli flakes

1 teaspoon anardana
(pomegranate powder)

1 tablespoon honey

2 tablespoons olive oil, plus extra
for frying

4 x 200g sirloin steaks, about
1.5cm thick

Knob of butter

Juice of 1 lemon

Handful of fresh mint leaves, finely
chopped

Handful of fresh coriander leaves,
finely chopped

Sea salt and black pepper, to taste

For the Raita

½ bunch of fresh coriander, leaves
finely chopped

½ bunch of fresh mint, leaves
picked and finely chopped

½ cucumber peeled, deseeded and
finely diced

300g full-fat Greek yoghurt

1 teaspoon cumin seeds,
dry-roasted and ground

½ teaspoon dried mint

Salt, to taste

The word *pasand* means 'preferred' or 'favourite' in Urdu, the language of Pakistan. These steaks are indeed one of my favourites! I often cook them after a busy day at work; they are incredibly easy to make and satisfy the whole brood. The marinade is an adaptation of an ancient Mughal recipe where strips of lamb are flattened with a mallet and fried with various spices.

Mix together the cumin, coriander, garlic, ginger, paprika, chilli flakes, anardana, honey and olive oil to make a marinade. Rub this marinade over both sides of the steaks and leave to rest for at least 30 minutes at room temperature.

Season the steaks generously with salt and pepper. Place a non-stick frying pan over a high heat until it is searing hot. Add the knob of butter to the pan with a drizzle of olive oil. Add the steaks to the hot pan, in two batches if necessary, and caramelise for 2 minutes on each side, to create a charred outer crust. Transfer the steaks to a baking sheet, cover tightly with foil and allow to rest for 10 minutes.

Meanwhile, make the raita. Mix the coriander and mint with the cucumber, yoghurt, cumin seeds and dried mint. Season to taste with salt.

Once the steak has rested, slice it into thin strips and dress with the lemon juice and chopped herbs. Serve immediately with the cucumber, coriander and mint raita.

 NB *Charring the steaks will create some smoke, so make sure you use an extractor fan or open a window.*

in Yoghurt Sauce
with Buttery Basmati Rice
Goshtaba Beef Meatballs

SERVES 4

For the Meatballs

400g minced beef (not too lean)
1 onion, roughly chopped
½ teaspoon ground cardamom
2 teaspoons ground ginger
1 teaspoon dried mint
2 teaspoons ground coriander
2 teaspoons fennel seeds
1 teaspoon ground cumin
1 teaspoon chilli flakes
Vegetable oil, for frying
Salt, to taste
Handful of fresh mint leaves, to garnish

For the Yoghurt Sauce

30g ready-made crispy fried onions (see Note)
1 teaspoon fennel seeds
1 teaspoon chilli flakes
250ml water
500g natural yoghurt
1 teaspoon dried mint
1 tablespoon cornflour
Salt, to taste

For the Rice

300g basmati rice
100g butter

I remember one summer holiday spent in a houseboat on the Dal Lake in Srinagar, Kashmir; Mum bought pashmina shawls, apples and walnuts from a vendor on a dinghy. I have fond memories of enjoying goshtaba with my family under the Kashmir moonlight at a roadside stall. It was a dish of fennel-scented meatballs in a perfumed mint and fennel yoghurt broth – just delightful. My version is an adaptation of the traditional recipe, and is a beautiful warming dish for a cold winter day.

First make the meatballs: put all the ingredients, except the vegetable oil and mint leaves, into a food processor or blender and whizz until the meat has roughly the texture of sausage meat. Transfer to a bowl and chill in the fridge for 30 minutes.

Using lightly oiled hands, shape the mixture into about 12 walnut-sized meatballs and place on a greased plate.

Drizzle some vegetable oil into a deep non-stick pan and fry the meatballs quickly over a medium-high heat to form a golden brown outer crust. Once a crust has formed, pour enough warm water into the pan to completely cover the meatballs. Put a lid on the pan and simmer over a medium heat for about 30–45 minutes. The meatballs should be tender and break easily with a fork, while the stock will have reduced down.

Meanwhile, make the yoghurt sauce. Put the crispy fried onions into a food processor or blender with the fennel seeds, chilli flakes and measured water and blitz to form a smooth onion paste. Pour the yoghurt into a large pan and whisk the yoghurt, off the heat, until it is very smooth. Add the onion paste and dried mint and whisk gently until the onion paste and yoghurt are combined. Now simmer the yoghurt sauce over the lowest heat for 20 minutes, stirring continuously with a whisk – increasing the temperature will cause the mixture to split, so be patient at this stage.

To thicken the sauce, blend the cornflour with a few tablespoons of water until it is smooth. Pour this cornflour mixture into the yoghurt sauce and keep stirring for the next 2–3 minutes – it should thicken up nicely to create a sauce with the consistency of double cream. Season with salt to taste.

Boil the rice in a large pan of salted water until just tender; drain thoroughly in a colander and transfer to a bowl. Add the butter to the hot rice and allow it to melt slowly. Stir only once with a fork, being careful to treat the rice gently.

While the rice is cooking, remove the cooked meatballs from the pan of liquid with a slotted spoon, gently drop them into the yoghurt sauce and simmer over a low heat for a final 5 minutes.

Serve the goshtaba meatballs with the buttery rice, garnished with a handful of mint leaves.

NB *I like to buy packets of ready-made fried onions – they are available from good supermarkets and Asian food stores and are a great shortcut when it comes to making sauces like the one above. They also work brilliantly as a garnish.*

Lamb Shanks
in Pomegranate & Date Syrup
with Aubergine & Chickpea Couscous

SERVES 4

2 tablespoons olive oil

1 onion, thinly sliced

5 cloves

1 cinnamon stick

3 star anise

1 tablespoon fennel seeds

1 teaspoon chilli flakes

2 thumb-sized pieces of ginger, unpeeled

4 French-trimmed lamb shanks (about 200–250g each)

3 dried limes

120g dates

2 tablespoons pomegranate molasses

Salt, to taste

For the Couscous

200g couscous

1 x 400g tin chickpeas, rinsed and drained

250ml hot beef stock

4 tablespoons olive oil

1 medium aubergine, cut into small cubes

Juice of ½ lemon

½ bunch of fresh flat-leaf parsley, finely chopped

Salt, to taste

This lamb shank recipe is a truly celebratory. The meat is soft, sweet and almost falling off the bone, while the fragrant date and pomegranate sauce is rich and perfectly spiced. While I completely appreciate that the Mughals would typically have eaten rice instead of couscous, I cannot deny that it is the perfect accompaniment here.

Heat the olive oil in a deep casserole dish and add the onion. Fry over a medium heat for about 5 minutes; when the onion starts turning golden, add the cloves, cinnamon, star anise, fennel seeds, chilli flakes and ginger. Cook the spices gently for a minute, being careful not to let them to burn.

Add the lamb shanks to the pan and brown them in the onions and spices, turning to brown all sides. Finally, add the dried limes and dates to the casserole dish with just enough warm water to cover the shanks (about 900ml). Increase the heat to bring the mixture to the boil, then cover with a lid and reduce the heat to medium-low. Allow the lamb to simmer for about 2 hours, or until it is tender to touch and practically falling off the bone.

Remove the casserole dish from the heat and allow to cool slightly. Gently remove the lamb shanks from the casserole dish with a slotted spoon and set aside. Strain the liquid in the casserole dish through a sieve, discarding the whole spices. Return the strained liquid to the casserole dish, add the pomegranate molasses and season to taste with salt. Place back over a medium heat to reduce the liquid to a sauce with the consistency of double cream.

Meanwhile, put the couscous and drained chickpeas into a bowl. Bring the stock to a boil and season with salt, then pour over the couscous.

Cover the bowl with cling film and allow to stand for 15 minutes. While the couscous is standing, heat half the olive oil in a frying pan over a medium-high heat and add the aubergine cubes. Fry for about 5 minutes, or until they have caramelised and softened. Fluff the couscous grains using a fork and drizzle with the remaining olive oil and the lemon juice. Mix the fried aubergine cubes into the couscous together with the chopped parsley.

Return the lamb shanks to the sauce and heat through gently. Serve with the aubergine and chickpea couscous.

Subhani Apricot Lamb Curry

with Crispy Potato Matchsticks & Sesame Flatbread

SERVES 4

1 garlic clove, finely grated

1 teaspoon grated ginger

600g boneless spring lamb, cut into small cubes

75–100g ghee or butter

3 onions, thinly sliced

½ teaspoon ground turmeric

1 teaspoon garam masala

1 teaspoon ground cumin

3 large ripe tomatoes, roughly chopped

1 teaspoon chilli flakes

350ml warm water

1 waxy potato, peeled

Vegetable oil, for frying

100g dried apricots, finely chopped

3 fresh apricots, stoned and thickly sliced

Salt, to taste

The Mughal Emperor Babur loved fruit so much that when conquests and battles forced him to move from central Asia to India, he craved his beloved apricots, pomegranates and apples.

Emperor Babur's life was documented in his own journal, the *Baburnama*. He speaks evocatively of the *subhani*, a dried variety of apricot found in the town of Marghinan in east Uzbekistan, as well as of fresh apricots. My inspiration for this dish comes from the description of the glorious apricot in the *Baburnama* – I use a combination of dried and ripe apricots to create a luscious fruity curry.

_____

Rub the garlic and ginger into the cubed lamb and allow to rest in the fridge for 30 minutes. Meanwhile, melt the ghee or butter in a large heavy-based pan. Add the onions and fry over a medium heat for 5–10 minutes, or until they are a deep golden brown. Add the cubed lamb to the onions together with the turmeric, garam masala and cumin. Stir well until the meat is brown, taking care not to let the spices catch.

Put the tomatoes into a food processor or blender with the chilli flakes and blitz to a purée. Add the puréed tomatoes to the lamb with the measured water and bring to the boil. Reduce the heat and simmer, uncovered, over a low-medium heat for about 45 minutes, or until the lamb is meltingly soft. Most of the liquid will have evaporated from the pan and oil will start bubbling up to the surface but if you find that

For the Sesame Flatbread

275g self-raising flour, plus extra for dusting

1 teaspoon sugar

1 teaspoon salt

1 tablespoon finely chopped fresh coriander

120ml warm milk

2 tablespoons vegetable oil

6 teaspoons black sesame seeds

2 tablespoons melted ghee or butter, for brushing

the lamb is not yet completely soft, add a little more warm water and continue to cook for another 15 minutes (the varying age of the lamb affects the cooking time, with spring lamb cooking much faster).

Meanwhile, prepare the sesame flatbread. Sift the flour into a large bowl (or the bowl of a stand mixer) and add the sugar, salt and chopped coriander. Mix the milk and oil in a jug and pour slowly into the flour. Knead by hand (or with a dough hook) for about 5 minutes until the dough is nice and elastic.

Form the dough into eight equal-sized balls. Dust the worktop with flour and roll out each dough ball until it is the approximate thickness of a £1 coin. Put onto a baking sheet lined with baking parchment, moisten the surface of each flatbread with a wet hand and sprinkle over the black sesame seeds. Cover with cling film and allow to rest for at least 30 minutes.

When the time is nearly up on the curry, cut the potato into thin slices and then cut each slice into long thin strips to form potato matchsticks. Heat vegetable oil in a pan until sizzling hot and deep-fry the matchsticks for a minute or two until they are golden and crisp. Drain on kitchen paper and sprinkle with salt.

To cook the flatbreads, place a large non-stick frying pan over a medium-high heat and add the flatbreads, a few at a time. Cook for about 3–4 minutes on each side until the bread is golden and cooked through. Brush the flatbreads with the ghee or butter as soon as they come out of the pan.

To finish the curry, add the dried apricots and simmer for a final 4–5 minutes. Season to taste with salt. Add the fresh apricot slices and remove from the heat, allowing the raw fruit to soften in the residual heat of the pan. Serve the apricot curry in large spoonfuls on top of the sesame flatbread and topped with the fried potato matchsticks.

Illustrated overleaf.

Stuffed with Spiced Mutton Mince & Sweet Garden Peas

Dopiaza Roasted Onions

SERVES 4–6

3 very large onions

Vegetable oil, for frying

400g minced mutton (or use minced lamb)

1 garlic clove, finely grated

1 teaspoon chilli flakes

½ teaspoon ground turmeric

½ teaspoon garam masala

½ teaspoon cumin seeds

1 x 400g tin chopped tomatoes

300ml water

150g garden peas, defrosted if frozen

50g sour cherries

1 tablespoon pomegranate molasses

30g softened butter

Salt, to taste

Dopiaza was a magnificent onion and meat curry that was enjoyed by the Mughals. Today it's still eaten across the Indian subcontinent, but particularly in the town of Hyderabad, where Mughal food remains immensely popular.

A close friend of our family used to make dopiaza curry extra special by adding lemon juice, dried berries and raw mangoes for tartness. In my version I use a mixture of pomegranate molasses and cranberries to enrich the dish and stuff the onions with minced mutton rather than making an onion-based curry. The soft onion flesh against the sour, salty mutton mince is quite incredible.

Trim the top and bottom of the onions and then cut each in half lengthways. Carefully separate the onion layers, keeping the larger outer ones (you can use the insides in another recipe). Blanch the large onion layers in a pan of boiling water for 2 minutes, remove with a slotted spoon and allow them to cool.

Heat a drizzle of vegetable oil in a large pan over a medium heat and add the minced mutton, garlic, chilli flakes, turmeric, garam masala and cumin seeds. Cook, stirring, for about 5 minutes until the meat is browned all over.

Put the chopped tomatoes into a food processor or blender with the measured water and blitz to a purée – add this tomato purée to the mince. Simmer over a medium heat for 20 minutes until the liquid has reduced by about two-thirds. Meanwhile, preheat the oven to 200°C (180°C fan), gas mark 6.

Fifth Mughal Emperor Shah Jahan (reigned from 1628–1658) watching an elephant fight with his two sons, as depicted in a watercolour painting by Bulaqi.

Allow the mince to cool slightly before adding the peas, sour cherries and pomegranate molasses. Season to taste with salt.

Fill each onion layer with the stuffing mixture, pulling the edges together to create a fat oval shape. Place the stuffed onions seam side down into an ovenproof dish. Rub the softened butter over the exposed surface of the onions and bake uncovered for approximately 30 minutes, or until the onions have softened completely and can be pierced easily with a knife. Serve with buttery rice, a crisp salad or simply on its own.

Lamb, Mint & Peas

SERVES 4

Bunch of fresh mint, leaves picked
½ bunch of fresh coriander
2 heaped teaspoons fennel seeds
2 heaped teaspoons anardana
(pomegranate powder)
1 teaspoon cumin seeds
1 green chilli
100g full-fat Greek yoghurt
Juice of 1 lemon
3 tablespoons olive oil
8–10 spring lamb chops, fat
trimmed
50g pea shoots
Handful of pomegranate seeds
500g fresh shelled peas

Could there be anything more quintessentially British than lamb, mint and peas? My Mughal-inspired take on a British classic uses fennel seeds, mint and a very special ingredient: anardana. This powdered dried pomegranate has a deep, tart flavour that is similar to sumac. It acts as a meat tenderiser and also cuts through the fat of the lamb chops. These would of course cook very well in a tandoor oven (the classic Mughal way of cooking) but a barbecue, griddle or grill will do just fine.

Put the mint leaves, coriander, fennel seeds, anardana, cumin seeds, green chilli, Greek yoghurt, most of the lemon juice and 2 tablespoons of the olive oil into a food processor or blender and blitz until smooth. Reserve a few teaspoons of this marinade and pour the remainder over the lamb chops. Set aside to rest for 30 minutes at room temperature (or the fridge if it is a very hot day).

Preheat the grill to its highest setting. Grill the chops for about 4 minutes each side, or until they look golden brown and charred at the edges. (Alternatively, preheat the oven to 220°C (200°C fan), gas mark 7, put the chops into a roasting tray, cover with foil and bake for 45 minutes until the meat is tender and succulent.)

Add a touch more lemon juice and the remaining tablespoon of olive oil to the reserved marinade and use this to dress the pea shoots. Add a handful of pomegranates seeds for colour and a burst of freshness.

Boil the fresh peas for 2 minutes and drain. Serve the peas with the lamb chops and pea shoot salad.

Lamb Braised
with Prunes & Rose Water

SERVES 4

50ml olive oil
2 onions, thinly sliced
1 cinnamon stick
1 bay leaf
1 teaspoon fennel seeds
1 teaspoon ground ginger
½ teaspoon ground turmeric
1 teaspoon chilli flakes
500g boneless lamb cubes
250ml warm water
100g prunes
2 tablespoons rose water
Dried rose petals, to garnish

Dried fruits and nuts were symbols of opulence and grandeur in the Mughal Empire. Prunes are sweet and dense, a perfect accompaniment to soft, sweet spring lamb. The addition of rose water adds a subtle perfume, making this a sophisticated dish that works so well with warm naan bread.

Add the olive oil to a large heavy-based pan and fry the onion over a low-medium heat for about 20 minutes until it turns a deep golden brown. Add the cinnamon stick, bay leaf, fennel seeds, ground spices and chilli flakes, stirring for a couple of minutes to prevent the onions and spices from catching.

Add the lamb to the pan and stir well until the meat has browned slightly and the onions look like they are breaking down. Add the measured water, cover the pan with a lid and allow the meat to simmer over a medium heat for 30 minutes, or until the lamb has softened completely. You may need to add a little more water to the pan if the lamb starts looking too dry before the 30 minutes are up, or if the lamb has not softened after 30–45 minutes of cooking.

Put the prunes into a food processor or blender with a tablespoon or two of water and blitz to a smooth purée. Stir the prune purée into the lamb and cook for a further 15–20 minutes until the sauce is thick, dark and glossy.

Remove the pan from the heat and add the rose water. Serve the lamb garnished with a handful of dried rose petals.

Leg of Lamb

Braised in Yoghurt with Turmeric
Roast Potatoes

1 x 1.6kg deboned leg of lamb (ask your butcher to debone for you)

700g full-fat Greek yoghurt

1 tablespoon garam masala

1 teaspoon chilli powder

1 teaspoon chilli flakes

80g grated ginger

12 garlic cloves, finely grated

700ml water

Juice of 1 lemon

Handful of chopped dried apricots

Handful of toasted chopped nuts, such as pistachios, almonds or pine nuts

Salt, to taste

For the Potatoes

1kg jersey royals or other new potatoes

2 tablespoons olive oil

75g melted butter

½ teaspoon ground turmeric

1 teaspoon cumin seeds

Sea salt, to taste

Who doesn't like their lamb cooked low and slow? This recipe produces the most soft, succulent lamb imaginable, and as the oven does all the work for you, hardly any prep is required! An excellent festive dish to enjoy with loved ones.

Put the flat piece of deboned lamb into a deep, wide roasting tray. Use a sharp knife to make some deep incisions in the meat – this will allow the marinade to penetrate into the lamb.

Combine the Greek yoghurt with the spices, ginger and garlic and then whisk in the measured water and lemon juice. Rub this yoghurt mixture over both sides of the lamb and allow it to marinate for at least 6 hours, preferably overnight. Preheat the oven to 150°C (130°C fan), gas mark 2.

Seal the roasting tray tightly with foil and roast in the oven for 4 hours. After this time remove the foil and check the lamb. If it is completely tender, carefully lift it from the roasting tray and place it on a platter, cover with foil and allow to rest. Alternatively, return the lamb to the oven for another hour.

Meanwhile, make a start on the potatoes. Cook the potatoes in a large pan of boiling salted water for about 10–12 minutes, or until a knife can just penetrate through the potato easily. Drain and set aside to steam dry and cool slightly. Crush the par-boiled potatoes with the palm of your hand to flatten them, and place them in a single layer on a greased baking sheet.

As soon as the lamb is out of the oven, increase the oven temperature to 220°C (200°C fan), gas mark 7. Mix together the olive oil, melted butter, turmeric and cumin seeds and pour over the potatoes, making sure they are all coated. Sprinkle generously with sea salt and roast for 30–45 minutes until they are crisp and golden brown at the edges and soft and fluffy in the centre. Turn the potatoes once during the cooking.

While the lamb is resting and the potatoes are cooking, prepare the yoghurt sauce. Transfer the juices in the bottom of the roasting tray to a food processor or blender – don't worry that they appear curdled as this is to be expected. Blitz the juices until smooth, then add them to a pan. Place the pan over a medium heat and whisk constantly to reduce the juices and form a thick, smooth yoghurt sauce.

To finish the dish, pour the reduced yoghurt sauce over the leg of lamb and top generously with the chopped apricots and toasted chopped nuts. Serve with the crispy turmeric potatoes.

Steamed Lamb Manty
with Tomato & Garlic Sauce

SERVES 4

300g minced lamb
1 small red onion, finely chopped
1 teaspoon cumin seeds
1 teaspoon grated ginger
1 garlic clove, finely grated
1 red chilli, finely diced
1 teaspoon garam masala
1 beaten egg
24 dim sum wrappers
Vegetable oil
Salt, to taste

To Serve

75ml sour cream, at room temperature
2 garlic cloves, finely grated
300ml tomato passata
50g butter
1 red chill, very finely chopped
½ teaspoon dried mint
½ teaspoon chilli flakes
Few fresh mint leaves, finely chopped

NB *To make your own dumpling wrappers, combine 350g plain flour with a teaspoon of salt, a beaten egg and enough water to form a pliable dough. Knead for 5 minutes and rest for 15–20 minutes before rolling out the dough thinly using a pasta machine or rolling pin. Cut the dough into squares and use as above.*

King Babur was the first Mughal emperor. Born in Uzbekistan, he was always extremely proud of his central Asian heritage. King Babur's kitchen records show that he enjoyed eating lamb manty, a dumpling dish that is still eaten today in Uzbekistan, Afghanistan and northern Pakistan. I use plenty of earthy spices to flavour the dumplings.

You will need about 24 dim sum wrappers (look for ones that are white in colour), available from good Asian food stores or large supermarkets.

Put the minced lamb into a bowl with the onion, cumin seeds, ginger, garlic, chilli, garam masala and beaten egg. Season the mince with plenty of salt and mix well to combine.

Spoon a teaspoonful of the lamb mince filling onto the centre of each dim sum wrapper and brush the exposed corners with water. Seal the dumpling by bringing the four corners of the dough square together and pinching tightly to seal the meat inside the dumpling. (You can freeze the unsteamed dumplings at this point.) Dip the base of each dumpling in vegetable oil and place onto a steaming basket set over a pan of boiling water. Steam the manty dumplings for about 8–10 minutes.

Meanwhile, prepare the sauces. Mix together the sour cream and garlic, season with a pinch of salt and set aside. Put the passata, butter, red chilli and a pinch of salt into a small pan and cook over a low heat until the sauce is thick and buttery.

To serve, arrange the steamed dumplings on a platter and spoon over the garlic sour cream and tomato sauce. Sprinkle over the dried mint and chilli flakes and top with the chopped mint. Enjoy immediately.

Roughan Josh

with Saffron Mash & Pickled Red Onion Salad

SERVES 4

1.5 litres water

10 cloves

700g boneless lamb (shoulder or leg), cubed

100g butter

2 large onions

3 garlic cloves, finely grated

2 teaspoons mild Kashmiri chilli powder

½ teaspoon ground turmeric

½ teaspoon ground cardamom

Pinch of saffron threads

Salt, to taste

For the Saffron Mash

75g butter

Good pinch of saffron threads

1kg Maris Piper potatoes, peeled and cut into chunks

4 tablespoons milk

Salt and black pepper, to taste

For the Pickled Red Onion Salad

1 red onion, thinly sliced into rings

Juice of 1 lemon

2 tablespoons cider vinegar

1 heaped teaspoon sugar

½ red chilli, thinly sliced

Salt, to taste

Rogan josh is, of course, a much-loved Indian takeaway dish. To my surprise and delight the Mughals are credited with the creation of this classic. However, I must say that the original version was vastly different – and in a very good way! It is creamy and fragrant without being overtly spicy and has a slightly thinner consistency. In fact, *roughan* means 'clarified butter' or 'fat' in Persian; this dish definitely does have a beautiful buttery note.

Put the measured water into a large pan and bring to the boil. Tie the cloves in a muslin cloth and add this to the boiling water together with the cubed lamb. Allow the lamb to simmer gently for about 30 minutes, occasionally removing any scum that rises to the surface with a ladle.

In a separate large pan, melt half the butter over a low heat, add the onions and fry gently until they turn a deep golden brown, about 20–25 minutes. Remove the onions from the heat, allow them to cool a little and then blitz to a purée in a food processor or blender (you may need to add a few tablespoons of warm water to loosen the purée). Return the onion purée to the pan, add the garlic, Kashmiri chilli powder, turmeric and cardamom, and stir for a minute or two.

Remove and discard the bag of cloves from the lamb and then add the lamb, together with the liquid it was simmering in, to the pan of onions. Simmer for another 30–45 minutes, or until the lamb is soft and falls apart easily.

Meanwhile, prepare the saffron mash. Melt the butter in a pan and add the saffron. Remove from the heat and allow the saffron to steep in the butter for at least 15 minutes until the butter changes colour to a vivid shade of yellow. Boil the potatoes in a large pan of salted water until cooked through, about 15 minutes.

While the potatoes are cooking, mix all the ingredients for the pickled red onion salad together in a bowl and set aside for at least 15 minutes before serving.

Once cooked, drain the potatoes thoroughly in a colander and then transfer to a large bowl. Add the saffron butter together with the milk and mash well, making sure there are no lumps. Season with plenty of salt and pepper to taste. Alternatively, you can use a potato ricer to create a smooth effect. Be cautious of overbeating, as you don't want the potatoes to have a gluey texture.

When the lamb has finished simmering, add the saffron and the remaining butter and stir until you have a sauce with the consistency of double cream. Season to taste with salt before serving with the saffron mash and pickled red onion salad.

Lamb Mince
in a Poppy Seed & Almond Sauce

SERVES 4

75ml olive oil

1 onion, finely chopped

3 garlic cloves, finely grated

1 tablespoon grated ginger

3 green chillies, finely chopped

1 teaspoon ground cinnamon

½ teaspoon ground cardamom

½ teaspoon ground turmeric

2 teaspoons ground coriander

750g minced lamb

2 tomatoes, chopped

350ml warm water

75g blanched skinless almonds

75g Greek yoghurt

1 tablespoon white poppy seeds

Salt, to taste

To Garnish

Handful of toasted flaked almonds

Handful of fresh mint leaves, finely chopped

Handful of fresh coriander leaves, finely chopped

During my research for this book, I stumbled upon an ancient Mughal text which described a leg of lamb being slow-roasted overnight in a white poppy seed and almond paste. The mouth-watering description inspired me to come up with this minced lamb dish, a sort of Mughal chilli con carne. White poppy seeds are an incredible ingredient, swelling as they cook to absorb the flavour of spices they are exposed to. The final result is just sublime!

———————————

Heat the oil in a large pan and add the onion, garlic, ginger and chillies. Fry over a medium heat for about 20–25 minutes until the onions are golden brown. Add the ground spices and mix well, taking care not to let them catch.

Add the minced lamb to the pan and stir to allow the meat to brown well with the onions and spices. Add the tomatoes and measured water and allow the mince to bubble away for 25 minutes.

Put the almonds, Greek yoghurt and poppy seeds into a food processor or blender and blitz to a smooth purée, then add this to the pan. Season to taste with salt, reduce the heat and simmer for a further 25 minutes. If the mixture appears too dry and is catching at the bottom of the pan, add another cup of warm water. The lamb will be cooked when it has a thick sauce-like consistency, is a dark golden brown colour and the fat starts rising to the surface.

Remove from the heat and scatter with the toasted flaked almonds and chopped mint and coriander. Serve immediately, with flatbreads of your choice, such a naan or pitta bread.

 NB *If you can't get hold of white poppy seeds, just leave them out; the recipe will still be completely delicious.*

Mutton & Lentil Haleem Stew

SERVES 8

100ml olive oil

1 onion, thinly sliced

500g boneless mutton, cubed (or use lamb)

3 garlic cloves, finely grated

1 tablespoon grated ginger

1–2 teaspoons chilli powder (depending on how spicy you like it)

1 teaspoon cracked black pepper

1 teaspoon ground cumin

1 teaspoon ground coriander

1 teaspoon garam masala

½ teaspoon ground cardamom

½ teaspoon ground turmeric

100g chana dal (yellow split lentils)

100g pearl barley

100g moong/mung dal (huskless split mung beans)

100g masoor dal (red split lentils)

100g urad dal (white huskless black gram lentils)

4 litres warm water

Salt, to taste

To Garnish

Handful of ready-made crispy fried onions

Handful of chopped fresh coriander

Fresh ginger, peeled and cut into julienne

Lemon wedges

When I was growing up, haleem signalled celebration – it was the centrepiece of any feast in our home. This rich, dense and flavoursome dish of lentils cooked slowly with meat was a favourite in the Court of the Mughal Emperor Akbar. I would save my appetite for this majestic dish, devouring platefuls with lemon juice, ginger, fried onions and warm naan bread. What a treat… my mouth waters just thinking about it. I use a pressure cooker to make my haleem. If you don't have one, you can prepare it as below using a large heavy-based pan instead, although you will need to cook it for about 4–5 hours to get the same deliciously soft texture!

Pour the oil into a pressure cooker and place over a medium heat. Once the oil is hot, add the sliced onion and fry until it is a deep golden brown. Add the mutton pieces to the pan followed by the garlic, ginger and all the spices. Stir for a few minutes to coat the meat in the spices.

Once the meat has started to colour, add all the lentils, pearl barley and the measured water and bring to the boil. Put the lid of the pressure cooker on the pan; when the pressure cooker starts whistling, reduce the heat to medium and leave to cook in the pressure cooker for 2 hours; every 30 minutes or so pick up the entire pressure cooker with your oven gloves and swirl it around gently to redistribute the ingredients.

When the time is up, remove the pressure cooker from the heat and allow to cool. Carefully remove the lid and stir the contents vigorously with a wooden spoon to break down the meat fibres and combine them with the lentils. Season with salt to taste. The final texture should be that of a thick, textured soup – if you prefer a thinner texture, add a little hot water.

Serve the haleem in deep bowls, garnished with crispy fried onions, fresh coriander, ginger julienne and lemon wedges, and with any flatbread of your choice.

Lamb & Potato Seekh Kebabs

SERVES 4–5

Vegetable oil, for greasing

1 large onion, roughly chopped

1 large potato, peeled and diced

6 garlic cloves, chopped

Thumb-sized piece of ginger, peeled and grated

3–6 green finger chillies (depending on how hot you like it)

500g minced lamb (not too lean)

1 tablespoon cumin seeds

1 heaped teaspoon ground coriander

3 tablespoons finely chopped fresh coriander

1 beaten egg

2–3 tablespoons melted butter or ghee

10 bamboo skewers soaked in water for a few hours (optional)

Salt, to taste

These kebabs are full of flavour and have the most wonderful moist texture. They are really quite fabulous in flatbreads, with salad or rice. The potato and onion tenderise the lamb and the final result is an incredibly soft, moreish meat. I cook them in the oven but on summer days you can also load the mince onto skewers and do them on a barbecue.

Preheat the oven to 220°C (200°C fan), gas mark 7 and lightly grease a baking sheet.

Put the onion into a food processor along with the potato, garlic, ginger and green chillies. Blitz the mixture until the potato and onion have broken down into really small fragments, smaller than grains of rice.

Add the minced lamb to the food processor and give the mince a quick blitz to combine with the potato and onion mixture. Tip the mixture into a large bowl and mix in the cumin seeds, ground coriander, fresh coriander and beaten egg and season with salt.

Rub your hands with a little oil – this will make it easy to shape the kebabs. Take a small portion of the mince and gently roll it out into a long kebab shape, about 3cm thick and 10cm long. You should get about 10 long kebabs, but you can make any shape you like, including small walnut-sized koftas or burger-style patties if you prefer. Thread the kebabs on to the skewers, if using.

Lay the kebabs on the greased baking sheet and brush over the melted butter or ghee. Transfer to the oven and bake for about 25–30 minutes. The kebabs will have cooked through and will be light golden brown on the outside. You can sear them in a very hot, dry non-stick pan if you want to achieve a darker, charred crust.

Poultry & Game

ughal cuisine developed in the most wonderful way during the reign of the Mughal Emperor Akbar. There was exquisite attention to detail and the very best produce was brought to the imperial kitchens from all over the vast and ever-expanding empire.

Ducks, quails and chickens were all reared in Mughal kitchen gardens. There are accounts of palace chickens being hand fed 'pellets flavoured with saffron and rose water' and being massaged daily with musk oil and sandalwood, all in an attempt to produce the most succulent chicken possible. I can only imagine how the poultry must have tasted after being given such love and attention.

As well as poultry from the imperial kitchen gardens, the Mughals enjoyed a variety of wild meats gathered through hunting. The memoirs of the Mughals are peppered with stories of the emperors hunting for cheetahs, rhinos, buffalo, waterfowl and deer; venison was cooked regularly by the imperial cooks.

Royal advisors would warn the emperors of the dangers of passion for women, alcohol and the hunt. But hunting remained a sign of power and masculinity and the emperors drew up rigorous annual hunting calendars. Emperor Akbar would use hunting parties as a way of gathering information about the state of the people and the army and so food and political relations became closely aligned.

Chicken Thigh & Sour Mango Curry

with Coriander Rice

SERVES 4

2 tablespoons olive oil

Handful of fresh curry leaves

1 teaspoon black mustard seeds

1 teaspoon cumin seeds

500g skinless and boneless chicken thighs, cut into bite-sized chunks

½ teaspoon ground turmeric

1 teaspoon mild chilli powder

1 teaspoon amchoor (mango powder)

1 x 400ml tin coconut milk

150g frozen or fresh raw green mango slices (skin on)

Salt, to taste

Handful of coriander leaves, to garnish

For the Coriander Rice

300g basmati rice

50g butter

Bunch of fresh coriander, leaves finely chopped

Handful of toasted coconut flakes

The Mughals were obsessed with mangoes – Emperor Akbar is even said to have cultivated 100,000 mango trees in celebration of this most glorious fruit. This dish is deliciously tart – I use unripe sour mangoes that can easily be bought frozen from Asian shops. But if you can't find these, use slices of the most unripe mango you can find together with the juice of half a lemon instead.

Pour the olive oil into a non-stick pan and place over a medium heat. Add the curry leaves, black mustard seeds and cumin seeds. When the spices start popping and sizzling, add the chicken thighs to the pan and allow the chicken to caramelise and brown all over.

Once the chicken thighs are golden, add the turmeric, chilli powder and amchoor, followed by the coconut milk. Finally, add the raw mangoes and allow to simmer for 15 minutes until the thighs are cooked through and the sauce has thickened.

Meanwhile, cook the rice in plenty of salted water, according to the packet instructions. When the rice has just cooked through but is still slightly al dente, drain it in a colander. Melt the butter in the pan that you cooked the rice in and add the finely chopped coriander and toasted coconut flakes. Toss the drained rice into the butter and stir to combine.

Season the curry to taste with salt. Scatter over the chopped fresh coriander before serving with the buttery coriander rice.

Smoked Chicken & Basil Kebabs

with Beetroot Basil Salad & Beetroot Buttermilk Raita

100g Greek yoghurt

1 teaspoon grated ginger

1 garlic clove, finely grated

2 handfuls of fresh basil leaves

1 tablespoon garam masala

1 tablespoon chilli flakes

1 tablespoon cumin seeds

Pinch of salt

800g skinless and boneless chicken thighs

1 tablespoon olive oil

1 small piece of coal, about 4 x 4cm (optional) – make sure it has not been doused with commercial lighter fluid

For the Salad and Raita

800g beetroot, trimmed (reserve and thinly slice the stalks)

70ml olive oil

Juice of ½ lemon

1 red chilli, finely diced

½ teaspoon cumin seeds

Handful of beetroot stalks (optional)

Generous handful of fresh basil leaves

200ml buttermilk

1 teaspoon ground cumin

Salt, to taste

Illustrated overleaf (from left to right):

Smoky Spiced Aubergine & Pomegranate Vol-au-vents; Smoked Chicken & Basil Kebabs; Beetroot Buttermilk Raita; Lemon & Rose Sherbet; and Honey-roasted Grapes, Labneh, Roasted Walnuts & Persian Herbs.

For as long as I can remember, it has been a tradition to organise a family barbecue each summer. We marinate the meat together the night before and the final result is beautifully tender, succulent, charred and feverishly smoky.

This dish uses a Mughal cooking technique called *dhuandaar* to impart the flavour of smoke into cooked chicken. While not essential for this dish, it is a really simple and effective way of bringing the barbecue flavour to your dishes any time of the year. All you need is a small piece of coal… intrigued?

Preheat the oven to 220°C (200°C fan), gas mark 7. Put the yoghurt into a food processor or blender together with the ginger, garlic, basil leaves, garam masala, chilli flakes, cumin seeds and salt. Blitz until you have a smooth, vibrant green purée and pour it all over the chicken. Cover with cling film and allow to marinate for at least 30 minutes.

Put the beetroot into a roasting tin and roast for about 30–45 minutes, or until a knife can slide through them easily. Remove from the oven and allow to cool before peeling away the skin. Cut three-quarters of the beetroot (about 600g) into thin slices and arrange on a platter. Make a dressing by combining the olive oil, lemon juice, half the diced red chilli, the cumin seeds and sliced beetroot stalks, if using, together in a pestle and mortar. Add the basil leaves and salt to taste and bruise lightly. Spoon this dressing over the sliced beetroot. To make the raita, grate the remaining beetroot and combine with the buttermilk, remaining diced red chilli, ground cumin and salt to taste.

To cook the chicken, place a griddle pan over a high heat and brush lightly with olive oil. Add the chicken thighs and griddle for 5–7 minutes on each side until cooked all the way through. Put the cooked chicken into a wide casserole dish with a heavy, tight-fitting lid. Put a metal tablespoon into the casserole dish, on top of the cooked chicken. Now take the piece of coal in some kitchen tongs and hold it directly over the gas flame on the hob until it catches (it will take at least 5 minutes for the coal to become really hot). Carefully place the glowing coal on the metal tablespoon. Working quickly, pour the oil onto the piece of coal: smoke will form immediately. Place the lid on the casserole dish and allow the smoke to infuse the chicken for about 15–20 minutes. Serve the smoked chicken with the beetroot salad and raita.

Rose-scented Chicken
& Rose Shorba with Saffron Rice

SERVES 6

For the Chicken Patties

750g minced chicken

2 tablespoons dried rose petals

4 tablespoons rose petal jam

½ red onion, finely diced

Handful of finely chopped fresh coriander

1 garlic clove, finely grated

1 teaspoon grated ginger

1½ teaspoons cumin seeds

½ teaspoon grated nutmeg

1 tablespoon anardana (pomegranate powder)

1 red chilli, finely diced

1 egg

1 teaspoon gram flour

Salt, to taste

Vegetable oil, for frying

When Babur, the first Mughal emperor, travelled through Persia and Afghanistan to rule over India, he brought camels loaded with musk and damask roses with him. His love for roses is epitomised in his own words:

My heart, like the bud of the red, red rose,
Lies fold within fold aflame,
Would the breath of even a myriad Springs,
Blow my heart's bud to a rose?

The love affair with roses was such that each one of Babur's daughters was given a rose-related name: Gulchihra (rose-cheeked), Gulrukh (rose-faced), Gulbadan (rose-body) and Gulrang (rose-colour). This dish celebrates the romance of roses in the Mughal era and I am certain it would have pleased Babur himself. It has a gentle floral undertone, but if you like the perfume of roses, feel free to increase the quantity of rose water to your heart's desire.

For the Shorba

1.2 litres light chicken stock

2 star anise

1 cinnamon stick

5–7 cloves

3 cardamom pods

Thumb-sized piece of fresh ginger, peeled

200g cooked chicken breast, shredded

100g butter

1 onion, finely chopped

(Turn over for more ingredients)

Combine all the ingredients for the chicken patties, except the oil, in a large bowl and mix well. Place in the fridge for about 45 minutes.

To make the shorba, pour the stock into a pan and add the star anise, cinnamon stick, cloves, cardamom pods and ginger and bring to the boil. Lower the heat and simmer for about 25 minutes, then remove and discard the spices and ginger and add the shredded chicken.

Meanwhile, melt the butter in a separate pan, add the onion and fry over a low-medium heat for 20–25 minutes. When the onions are a deep golden brown, add the cumin seeds, turmeric and Kashmiri chilli powder and fry lightly to release the flavours. Add this onion and spice mixture to the pan of stock and stir to combine. Blend the cornflour with a few tablespoons of water to form a very smooth paste.

1 teaspoon cumin seeds

½ teaspoon ground turmeric

1 teaspoon mild Kashmiri chilli powder

1 tablespoon cornflour

3 tablespoons rose water

Juice of ½ lemon

3 tablespoons finely chopped fresh coriander

Salt, to taste

For the Saffron Rice

400g basmati rice

100g butter

Generous pinch of saffron threads

4 teaspoons rose water

Pour this paste into the shorba and bring the mixture to the boil, stirring gently. The shorba with thicken immediately.

To prepare the rice, preheat the oven to 200°C (180°C fan), gas mark 6 and wash the rice thoroughly in a sieve until the water runs clear. Bring a large ovenproof pan of salted water to the boil, add the rice and cook for three-quarters of the cooking time given on the packet, or until the rice is almost cooked but still has some bite. Meanwhile, melt the butter in a separate pan, add the saffron and allow it to steep in the melted butter. Drain the rice thoroughly, return to the pan and pour over the saffron butter. Sprinkle over the rose water, cover the pan with a lid and allow to steam in the oven for 15 minutes until the rice is cooked through.

While the rice is in the oven, shape the chicken mixture into small flat patties using lightly oiled hands. Pan-fry in vegetable oil over a medium heat for a few minutes on each side until cooked through.

To finish the shorba, add the rose water, lemon juice, chopped coriander and salt to taste just before serving with the chicken patties and saffron rice.

Onion & Saffron Roast Chicken Drumsticks

with Sweet Cucumber Salad

2 large onions, roughly chopped

3 garlic cloves, finely grated

1 tablespoon grated ginger

2 green chillies

1 tablespoon garam masala

75ml vegetable oil

Generous pinch of saffron threads

50ml warm milk

750g chicken drumsticks, skin removed

Salt, to taste

For the Cucumber Salad

1 small cucumber

1 teaspoon sugar

½ teaspoon salt

1 tablespoon white wine vinegar

Juice of ½ lemon

½ teaspoon chilli flakes

Handful of chopped fresh mint leaves

Sweet caramelised onions and aromatic yellow-hued saffron make the most deeply satisfying Mughal marinade for chicken. The cool, sharp cucumber slices are a fantastically light and refreshing accompaniment. The marinade would work just as well on chicken thighs or breast pieces if you prefer, or even a whole spatchcocked chicken.

———————————————

Put the onions, garlic, ginger, green chillies and garam masala into a food processor or blender and blitz with just enough water to form a smooth purée. Heat the oil in a pan, add the onion purée and cook over a medium heat, stirring regularly, until it turns a golden brown colour, about 20–30 minutes.

Preheat the oven to 220°C (200°C fan), gas mark 7 and line a roasting tray with foil.

Dissolve the saffron threads in the warm milk and add this to the cooked onion purée. Allow the mixture to cool and add salt to taste, then rub this onion and saffron marinade all over the chicken drumsticks. Tip the chicken and any leftover marinade into the lined roasting tray and seal the roasting tray tightly with more foil. Bake in the oven for 30 minutes, then remove the foil, baste the chicken with the juices at the bottom of the pan and return to the oven, uncovered, for a further 15–20 minutes.

Cut the cucumber in half lengthways, scoop out the seeds, then slice into chunky semicircles about 1cm thick. Whisk all the remaining ingredients together to make a dressing and pour this over the cucumber. Serve immediately, with the roasted chicken drumsticks.

Chicken Stuffed with Minced Lamb

with Barberry Chutney

SERVES 4

75g softened unsalted butter

30g barberries (see Note)

1 whole corn-fed chicken, about 1.4kg

1 tablespoon olive oil, plus extra for rubbing

250g minced lamb

1 teaspoon cumin seeds

1 teaspoon garam masala

½ teaspoon chilli flakes

½ teaspoon ground cinnamon

½ teaspoon grated nutmeg (optional)

25g pine nuts, toasted

50g basmati rice, cooked in boiling water for 5 minutes

Salt, to taste

For the Barberry Chutney

60g barberries, soaked in warm water for 15 minutes

4 tablespoons tamarind paste

1 teaspoon mild chilli powder

2 tablespoons sugar

Salt, to taste

This recipe will become your go-to dish when you want to impress your friends and relatives; it has certainly impressed everyone who dines at my home! The Mughals did not hesitate to combine chicken and lamb in dishes and this recipe is a classic example. The sharp, sweet barberries and earthy pine nuts are a wonderful way of harmonising the flavours of the two meats.

First mix the softened butter with the barberries until combined. Pat the chicken dry with a piece of kitchen paper and carefully stuff the barberry butter under the skin of the chicken, taking care not to tear the skin.

Heat the olive oil in a large frying pan and place over a medium heat. Add the minced lamb to the pan and cooked until brown, breaking up the mince a little with a wooden spoon. Add the cumin seeds, garam masala, chilli flakes, cinnamon, nutmeg, if using, and toasted pine nuts. Add the parboiled rice to the mince, season generously with salt and allow the mixture to cool.

Preheat the oven to 200°C (180°C fan), gas mark 6. Stuff the mince filling into the neck cavity of the chicken. You now need to seal in the filling as best you possibly can: there is no set way of doing this; if you are not experienced with trussing chickens do not panic. Just take a length of butchers' string and tie the chicken legs together as closely as possible so that the cavity of the bird is not exposed.

Rub olive oil over the surface of the stuffed chicken and sprinkle generously with salt. Put the chicken into a deep roasting tin and seal tightly with plenty of foil. Roast for 15 minutes, then lower the heat to 180°C (160°C fan), gas mark 4 and roast for a further 1 hour.

Baqi Beg Chaghaniani paying homage to Babur on the banks of the Oxus river in Central Asia, as depicted in the *Baburnama*.

Remove the foil from the roasting tray and baste the chicken with the buttery juices that have collected at the bottom of the pan. Return the chicken to the oven and increase the heat to 200°C (180°C fan), gas mark 6. Roast for a further 15 minutes, or until the skin has browned nicely. Allow the chicken to rest for 20 minutes before serving.

For the chutney, drain the soaked barberries and add to a food processor or blender with all the remaining ingredients. Add a few tablespoons of cold water and blend to a smooth paste. Transfer to a small pan and allow it warm very gently before serving with the stuffed chicken.

 NB *If you cannot get hold of barberries, try using sour cherries as an alternative.*

Malai Chicken Bites

800g boneless chicken (breast or thigh), cut into bite-sized chunks

1 tablespoon melted ghee or butter, for basting

For the Marinade

1 tablespoon gram flour

75g cheddar cheese

100ml single cream

100g full-fat Greek yoghurt

2 tablespoons finely chopped fresh coriander leaves

Juice of ½ lemon

1 teaspoon finely chopped green chillies

1 teaspoon chilli flakes

1 teaspoon dried fenugreek leaves

2 teaspoons grated ginger

6 garlic cloves, finely grated

2 tablespoons vegetable oil

1 teaspoon papaya paste meat tenderiser (optional)

Salt, to taste

The Mughals often marinated their meat in curds before roasting on spits and in tandoors. This moist, luxurious and creamy spiced 'malai' marinade makes a really delicious chicken dish, the perfect accompaniment to flatbreads and salads or even on its own as a delicious canapé. The cooking time will vary slightly depending on the size of your chicken cubes, but be wary of overcooking chicken breast.

First make the marinade. Put the gram flour into a dry frying pan over a medium heat and allow the flour to toast for a few minutes and become golden brown. Tip into a large bowl along with all the remaining ingredients and stir well to form a creamy marinade.

Add the chicken pieces to the bowl, turning to coat in the marinade. Cover with cling film and leave to marinate in the fridge for 1–24 hours (the longer you leave it the more tender the chicken will be). When you are ready to cook, preheat the oven to 200°C (180°C fan), gas mark 6.

Arrange the chicken pieces in a single layer on a baking tray along with all the marinade and roast for 20–25 minutes. After this time check the chicken by cutting through one of the pieces; the juices should run clear and the chicken will be moist and cooked through. The marinade will have become golden and caramelised on the edges of the chicken pieces. Baste the chicken pieces with the melted ghee or butter and allow to rest, covered with foil, for a few minutes before serving.

 NB These malai chicken bites will cook just as well on the barbecue, or under a hot grill for 12–15 minutes, turning once during cooking. Papaya paste meat tenderiser can be bought from Asian shops or online and is one of my secret ingredients: it helps make the most tender, juicy kebabs imaginable and is particularly useful when you don't have time to marinate overnight.

Peshawar-style Turkey Chapli Kebab

with Burnt Tomatoes & Buttery Rice

SERVES 4

500g minced turkey

1 beaten egg

1 soft-boiled egg

1 tomato, deseeded and finely diced

1 red onion, finely chopped

2 green chillies, finely chopped

3 teaspoons anardana (pomegranate powder)

1 teaspoon ground coriander

1 tablespoon cumin seeds, dry-roasted and lightly crushed

1 teaspoon chilli flakes

1 teaspoon hot paprika

4 tablespoons finely chopped fresh coriander

Salt, to taste

Olive oil, for frying

For the Tomatoes and Rice

300g basmati rice

16 small vine tomatoes

Olive oil, for brushing

50g salted butter

Sea salt, to taste

Chapli kebabs are one of the most popular dishes in the streets of Peshawar in north Pakistan and in parts of Afghanistan. The word *chapli* literally means 'slipper' in Urdu and traditionally the kebabs are flat and slightly ovular shaped, much like the front part of a shoe.

Although they are usually made with beef or lamb, I love cooking them with turkey – a lean, versatile and affordable meat.

Put all the kebab ingredients into a bowl, except the olive oil. Use a fork to mix all the ingredients together, making sure that the soft-boiled egg is well incorporated into the mince (the combination of raw and soft-boiled egg makes the cooked chapli kebabs more tender). Using lightly oiled hands, divide the mixture into eight and shape into flat patties, about 8cm in diameter and 1cm thick.

Bring a pan of water to the boil and preheat the grill to high. Cook the basmati rice according to the packet instructions; meanwhile, brush the tomatoes with olive oil and sprinkle with sea salt. Grill until the skins char and start bursting and the tomatoes soften.

When you are ready to cook the kebabs, drizzle a little olive oil into a non-stick pan and place over a medium-high heat. Fry the turkey kebabs for a few minutes on each side until they are golden on the outside and just cooked through (cooking for too long will dry the mince out completely, so take care to not overcook).

Drain the cooked rice thoroughly and return to the pan with the butter. Stir briefly with a fork, just to melt the butter into the steaming rice. Serve with the turkey kebabs and roasted tomatoes.

Stewed Poussin
with Saffron & Butter Beans

SERVES 2

100g butter

2 tablespoons olive oil

2 spatchcocked poussins, about 250g each (see Note)

2 large onions, thinly sliced

2 teaspoons grated ginger

4 garlic cloves, finely grated

½ teaspoon ground cardamom

3 bay leaves

1 teaspoon hot paprika

1 teaspoon mild Kashmiri chilli powder

500ml chicken stock

1 x 400g tin butter beans, rinsed and drained

Generous pinch of saffron threads

Salt, to taste

Handful of finely chopped fresh coriander, to garnish

I absolutely adore this dish; I love eating the leftovers the next day for lunch with a slice of crusty bread. I am really not sure what makes this dish so magical. Perhaps it is the opulence of saffron? Or the soft, fall-off-the-bone poussin? Poussins are young chickens, giving wonderfully tender yet flavourful meat and are perfect for a special meal for two.

Melt the butter in a 30cm shallow cast-iron casserole dish placed over a medium-high heat and drizzle in the olive oil. Pat the spatchcocked chicken dry with kitchen paper and place the chicken skin-side down into the fat. Allow the skin of the poussin to caramelise (aim for as dark brown a colour as possible) and then remove from the casserole dish and set aside.

Add the sliced onions to the casserole dish and fry for about 15–20 minutes until they are soft and starting to turn golden at the edges. Add the ginger, garlic, cardamom, bay leaves, paprika and Kashmiri chilli powder to the golden onions and stir well.

Return the spatchcocked poussins to the casserole dish, skin-side up, and pour in the chicken stock, adding more water if needed to come about two-thirds up the side of the poussins. Bring the mixture to the boil, then cover with a lid, reduce the heat and simmer for about 30 minutes. After 30 minutes remove the lid and add the butter beans, saffron and salt to taste. Simmer for a final 30 minutes, or until the chicken is soft to touch and practically falling off the bone. Garnish with plenty of coriander and serve with crusty bread.

 NB *Spatchcocking is a technique to remove the backbone, making it possible to flatten the bird and thereby speed up the cooking time. You can ask your butcher to do this for you but it's pretty easy to do yourself: place the bird breast-side down on a board. Use kitchen scissors to cut up along each side of the backbone to remove it. Turn the bird over, open it out and flatten the breastbone by pressing down with the heel of your hand.*

Masala Livers on Toast

with Pickled Ginger, Coriander & Crispy Onions

SERVES 2 GENEROUSLY

500g chicken livers

3 tablespoons full-fat Greek yoghurt

1 garlic clove, finely grated

1 teaspoon garam masala

1 teaspoon ground cumin

½ teaspoon chilli powder

4 tablespoons olive oil

Salt, to taste

Toasted sourdough, to serve

To Garnish

Thumb-sized piece of fresh ginger, peeled

Juice of ½ lemon

Handful of chopped fresh coriander

Handful of ready-made crispy fried onions (see Note on page 69)

When I was a child, Sunday brunch was always spicy livers on toast. They are full of flavour, take minutes to prepare and are a great source of nutrients, particularly iron. I use chicken livers here, but you can use duck liver, calf or lamb's liver – the same cooking principles will apply.

First prepare the ginger for the garnish. Cut the ginger into thin slices and then cut each slice into julienne. Pour over the lemon juice and allow the ginger to soften for about 15 minutes.

Rinse the livers in cold water and trim away any membranes. Pat the livers dry with kitchen paper and put into a non-metallic bowl. Add the Greek yoghurt, garlic, garam masala, ground cumin and chilli powder and mix well.

Heat the oil in non-stick pan until it is very hot. Add the livers to the oil and fry for about 4–5 minutes, stirring frequently to brown the livers all over. Sprinkle over salt to taste. Remove the livers from the pan when they are golden on the outside, soft and very slightly pink in the centre. Allow to rest for a few minutes before serving on slices of toasted sourdough. Garnish with the pickled ginger, fresh coriander and crispy fried onions. Enjoy immediately.

NB *Pickled ginger, coriander and fried onions are an authentic Pakistani garnish for meat-based dishes, but you can keep things simple with a wedge of lemon and any of your favourite herbs.*

with Spiced Plums & Caramelised Walnuts
Roast Kashmiri Duck

SERVES 4

1 whole duck, about 2kg
3 tablespoons olive oil
2 onions, thinly sliced
1 heaped teaspoon grated ginger
1 cinnamon stick
½ teaspoon ground turmeric
1 teaspoon cumin seeds
1 teaspoon garam masala
1 teaspoon fennel seeds
1 teaspoon chilli flakes
400g unripe plums, halved and stoned
2 heaped teaspoons sugar
Juice of 2 large oranges
300ml pomegranate juice
1 tablespoon honey
100g walnuts
Sea salt, to taste

It may not come as a surprise that I have always been fond of reading cookery books. As a child, I remember reading an evocative description of a Kashmiri family enjoying a picnic of braised duck with sour plums and walnuts in the Mughal-designed gardens of Srinagar, Kashmir. I have recreated this recipe in my own style.

Remove the giblets from the duck cavity and pat the skin dry with kitchen paper. Prick the skin of the duck all over with a toothpick; this will help the fat render off during the cooking process. Put the duck on a metal rack placed into a deep roasting tray, season generously with sea salt and roast in the oven for 1¼ hours. The fat will render down and pool at the bottom of the deep roasting dish.

Meanwhile, heat 2 tablespoons of the olive oil in a pan, add the sliced onions and fry over a low-medium heat for 20–25 minutes until they turn golden brown. Add the ginger, cinnamon, turmeric, cumin seeds, garam masala, fennel seeds and chilli flakes. Stir well to release all the flavours from the spices, making sure they don't catch on the bottom of the pan. Add the plums, sugar, orange juice and pomegranate juice. Allow the mixture to simmer for a few minutes and then remove from the heat and pour into a large ovenproof dish.

Remove the duck from the oven and carefully place it on top of the plum sauce. Return to the oven for a further 25 minutes. Just before the duck is ready, put the remaining tablespoon of olive oil into a small non-stick pan with the honey and place over a medium-low heat. Add the walnuts and allow them to caramelise lightly.

Serve the roasted duck and plum sauce with the caramelised walnuts. The plums will be soft but still keeping their shape and the duck will be crisp-skinned and moist.

NB *If you can't get hold of duck, this spiced plum sauce also works beautifully with roast chicken.*

Honey & Cardamom Quails

with Spiced Figs & Bulgur Wheat

SERVES 4

4 quails, about 250g each (skin on)

50g butter, melted

2 tablespoons blossom honey

1 tablespoon pomegranate molasses

1½ teaspoons chilli flakes

½ teaspoon ground cardamom

1 teaspoon cumin seeds, dry-roasted and ground

8 fresh figs, halved lengthways

250g bulgur wheat

Handful of soft dried figs, chopped

50g walnuts, chopped

150g pomegranate seeds

1 teaspoon chilli flakes

Juice of ½ lemon

2 tablespoons olive oil

Salt

If you have never tried quail before, this recipe is a fabulous starting point. The soft, sweet figs with perfectly cooked gamey quail make a dish that is utterly mouth-watering and an excellent dinner party dish as it is so quick to put together.

———————————

Preheat the oven to 220°C (200°C fan), gas mark 7.

Remove the quails from the fridge to allow them to come to room temperature and pat dry with kitchen paper.

Pour the melted butter into a bowl and add the honey, pomegranate molasses, chilli flakes, cardamom, ground cumin and salt to taste. Mix until well combined and then rub two-thirds of this marinade over the quails and the remaining third over the halved figs.

Place both the figs and quails in a roasting tray and roast in the oven for 20–25 minutes. The quails should be golden and caramelised with the juices running clear from the flesh.

Meanwhile, cook the bulgur wheat according to the packet instructions; drain thoroughly and put into a serving dish. Add the chopped dried figs, walnuts, pomegranate seeds, chilli flakes, lemon juice and olive oil. Stir to combine and season to taste with salt. Serve with the quails and roasted figs.

Fall off-the-bone Rabbit

in Garlic & Saffron Sauce

SERVES 4

100g butter

3 onions, thinly sliced

1 rabbit, about 1.2kg, jointed into 8 pieces (ask your butcher)

5 garlic cloves, peeled but left whole

3 bay leaves

3 star anise

Good pinch of saffron threads

½ teaspoon ground cumin

1 teaspoon chilli flakes

Juice of ½ lemon

2 tablespoons chopped fresh flat-leaf parsley

Salt, to taste

Toasted sourdough, to serve

When Emperor Babur invaded India, he overthrew King Lodhi of Hindustan. Babur's kindness led him to employ King Lodhi's cooks in his own kitchen. This proved to be a huge mistake as they tried to poison his rabbit and saffron stew. Luckily Emperor Babur survived; needless to say, the cooks did not! My rabbit and saffron dish cooks slowly over a low heat to create beautifully tender meat. It is just delicious with toasted sourdough or any flatbread of your choice.

Melt the butter in a shallow cast-iron casserole dish (about 30cm in diameter) placed over a medium heat and add the onions. Cook, stirring occasionally, until the onions turn a deep golden brown colour.

Pat the rabbit pieces dry with kitchen paper and add to the casserole dish. Increase the heat and cook the rabbit pieces until browned all over. It is essential that the rabbit and onions are well coloured at this stage.

Add the garlic cloves to the casserole dish with the bay leaves, star anise, saffron, cumin and chilli flakes. Add just enough warm water to cover the rabbit (about 750ml) and bring to the boil. Cover with a lid and reduce the heat to the lowest setting. Simmer for about 1½ hours, checking it every 30 minutes or so to make sure that the liquid has not evaporated completely and topping up with small amounts of warm water if required.

After 1½ hours of simmering, remove the lid from the casserole dish and cook for a final 20–30 minutes until the rabbit is completely tender and almost falling off the bone. Finish the dish by stirring through the lemon juice and chopped parsley. Season to taste with salt and serve with toasted sourdough bread.

Emperor's Venison Shami Kebabs

with Mint & Tomato Salad

SERVES 4–6

3 tablespoons olive oil, plus extra for frying

1 small onion, finely chopped

500g minced venison

100g chana dal (yellow split lentils), soaked for 2–24 hours

1 garlic clove, finely grated

1 teaspoon cumin seeds

1 teaspoon dried fenugreek leaves

1 teaspoon chilli flakes

1 teaspoon coriander seeds

4 cardamom pods, bruised with a rolling pin

1 bay leaf

½ teaspoon ground turmeric

1 teaspoon ground ginger

½ teaspoon coarsely ground black pepper

500ml warm water

1 tablespoon Greek yoghurt

1 beaten egg

Salt, to taste

The shami kebab is a rather unique kebab where minced meat is cooked with lentils and then blitzed in a food processor so that it has the texture of pâté. It was rumoured to have been invented for Mughal princes who lost their teeth from overindulgence, but still craved kebabs. While I cannot comment on whether there is any truth in this story, I do think it captures the imagination.

———————————

Pour the olive oil into a large pan and place over a medium heat. Add the onion and cook, stirring, for 5 minutes. When the onions have become translucent but not yet coloured, add the minced venison and stir vigorously to break up the meat and brown it evenly.

Drain the chana dal and add it to the pan with the garlic, whole spices and ground turmeric, ginger and pepper. Add the measured warm water and bring to a simmer. Cook over a medium heat for about 1 hour, or until the lentils are completely soft and all the moisture has evaporated from the pan. If the lentils are still a little firm, add more water to the pan and continue to cook until they break down when pressed between your fingertips (the varying age and soaking time of the lentils will mean they cook at slightly different speeds).

Allow the mixture to cool, then remove and discard the bay leaf and cardamom pods. Season with salt to taste. Transfer the venison mixture to a food processor or blender, add the yoghurt and blitz until smooth. Chill in the fridge for 30 minutes.

A miniature painting on ivory of fifth Mughal Emperor Shah Jahan, who reigned from 1628 to 1658.

For the Mint & Tomato Salad

2 large ripe tomatoes, thinly sliced

1 red onion, thinly sliced into rings

Bunch of fresh mint, leaves picked

2 tablespoons olive oil

Juice of ½ lemon

½ teaspoon black pepper

½ teaspoon cumin seeds, dry-roasted

½ teaspoon chilli flakes

Meanwhile, prepare the salad. Arrange the tomato and onion slices in a serving dish. Slice the mint leaves into thin strips and scatter over the tomatoes and onions. Whisk together the olive oil, lemon juice, black pepper, cumin seeds and chilli flakes to make a dressing and drizzle this over the tomatoes and onion.

Take the chilled venison mixture and form into 12 small patties. Heat a little olive oil in a non-stick frying pan over a low heat. Dip each patty in the beaten egg and add to the hot pan, in batches of two or three at a time. Fry for a few minutes on each side to create a golden brown crust, turning very carefully. Serve with the tomato and mint salad.

Fish & Seafood

when the Mughals moved from central Asia to India, they were exposed to a wide array of freshwater fish, which they completely fell in love with. Babur, the first Mughal emperor, was thought to be particularly fond of fish, which allegedly agreed with him more than beef and lamb.

But the symbolism of fish extended to beyond just the imperial dining table. When the Mughal emperors wished to bestow the highest possible honour upon a noble, they were awarded the 'rank of fish', the so-called *Mahi-o-Marati*. The fish was one of the nine royal ensigns symbolising the Mughal emperors' conquest of the world. The Mughal fish standard was placed horizontally on the point of spears made of gilded copper as part of grand processions.

I remember my great uncle visiting my grandmother in her home in Lahore. He would bring us huge quantities of a freshwater fish called khaga, a variety of catfish. My grandmother would marinate the fish immediately with slices of lemon before cooking it in a rich, aromatic spiced tomato and fish broth. We would all sit at the table and carefully pick the fish off the fine bones, devouring its soft, oily flesh with boiled rice.

The imperial cooks were also particularly keen to ensure that fish smelt fresh, so they often marinated it in citrus juice before cooking it in an array of fragrant spices. The tradition of marinating fish in lemon juice still lives on today as the heat of the Indian subcontinent makes fish perish particularly quickly. In line with this tradition, the recipes in this chapter of *Khazana* use citrus quite heavily.

In a way, it is quite difficult to relate the species of fish found in the Indian subcontinent (of which there are thousands) to the fish found in the cold waters of the North Sea and Atlantic. I have for the most part used fish that are readily available in the UK in this chapter. But if you can get hold of freshwater Indian fish, do not hesitate to use them for these recipes.

with Brown Sauce
& Spicy Chips
Sea Bream Pakoras

75g gram flour

75g cornflour

½–1 teaspoon chilli powder

½ teaspoon baking powder

Good pinch of salt

Juice of 1 lemon

1 tablespoon cumin seeds

1 tablespoon coriander seeds

8 sea bream fillets (skin on)

For the Brown Sauce

200g tamarind pulp

100g stoned dates

150ml water

70g jaggery (or use muscovado sugar)

1 teaspoon chilli flakes

1 teaspoon salt

½ teaspoon garam masala

½ teaspoon ground ginger

For the Spicy Chips

500g Maris Piper potatoes

½ teaspoon chaat masala

Vegetable oil, for frying

Fish, chips and brown sauce? Well yes, this recipe is essentially my interpretation of the much-loved classic British dish. My late grandmother, a truly talented cook, always felt a little disappointed by fish and chips: 'They are just a little bland', she would lament! And while we all disagreed fervently, I cannot help but admit that this sexy, spiced-up version of fish and chips brings an old classic straight into the twenty-first century.

First make the batter. Put the gram flour and cornflour into a bowl together with the chilli powder, baking powder and salt. Slowly pour in the lemon juice and just enough water to form a batter that has the consistency of double cream. Grind the cumin seeds and coriander seeds in a pestle and mortar until they start breaking down and whisk into the batter, making sure there are no lumps in the batter. Set aside until needed.

To make the brown sauce, put all the ingredients into a pan and place over a low-medium heat. Simmer gently for about 30 minutes, stirring occasionally, until the sauce has thickened and has the consistency of brown sauce. Pass the sauce through a sieve for a smooth result. The sauce will also thicken a little as it cools.

Cut the potatoes into thick chunky chips about 1cm thick (you can keep the skin on for extra texture). Heat vegetable oil in a deep fryer to a temperature of 140°C. Fry the chips for 8–10 minutes, then remove them and drain on kitchen paper. Allow them to cool: the chips will be soft but not coloured at this stage.

Increase the temperature of the oil to 180°C. Pat the sea bream fillets dry with kitchen paper and dip them gently into the pakora batter. Deep-fry the fish pakoras in batches for 4–5 minutes until the batter is crisp and golden brown and the fish is cooked through. Remove from the oil and drain on kitchen paper.

Deep-fry the chips in the hot oil a second time until they are crisp and golden. Drain on kitchen paper and sprinkle with the chaat masala.

Serve the sea bream pakoras with the chips and brown sauce.

Citrus Semolina Fried Sardines

with Preserved Lemon Relish

SERVES 4

1 garlic clove, finely grated

1 teaspoon mild Kashmiri chilli powder

1 teaspoon hot paprika

Zest and juice of 1 lemon

2 teaspoons olive oil

500g fresh sardine fillets

2 eggs

75g fine semolina

75g rice flour

1 tablespoon finely chopped fresh dill

1 tablespoon finely chopped fresh coriander leaves

Salt, to taste

Vegetable oil, for deep-frying

For the Preserved Lemon Relish

100g preserved lemons, halved and pips removed

2 red or green tomatoes

1 large green chilli (mild strength)

3 tablespoons finely chopped fresh coriander leaves

2 tablespoons roughly chopped fresh dill

2 tablespoons olive oil

1 teaspoon sugar

My dearest and most beloved grandfather, Nana abu, adored tinned sardines! When he knew that we were due to visit him in the Easter holidays, he would specifically request that we packed a few tins of sardines in our suitcase. Nana abu would squeeze lemon juice over the sardines and eat them on toast and I'm certain that my fondness for sardines stems from this precious memory of my grandfather. They remain one of the most inexpensive fresh fish, and take incredibly well to citrus.

Whisk together the garlic, chilli powder, paprika, lemon juice and olive oil in a small bowl and then rub all over the sardines. Set aside in the fridge to marinate for 15 minutes.

Meanwhile, make the relish. Put the preserved lemons into a food processor or blender with the tomatoes and green chilli and blitz to a coarse purée. Transfer to a bowl and stir in the coriander, dill, olive oil and sugar. Stir well and leave the relish to rest.

Beat the eggs in a wide bowl. Put the semolina, rice flour, lemon zest and chopped herbs in a tray, season generously with salt and mix thoroughly. Now start the production line: dip the sardines into the egg followed by the flour mixture, making sure they are completely coated.

Heat the vegetable oil in a large pan over a high heat until a pinch of semolina sizzles in the hot oil. Deep-fry the sardines, in batches if necessary, for a few minutes until they are crisp and golden. Drain on kitchen paper. Drizzle the preserved lemon relish over the fried fish and serve immediately, with buttered rice, a simple salad or flatbreads.

Tilapia & Caramelised Onion Masala

with Barberry Rice

SERVES 4

325g basmati rice

100ml olive oil, plus extra for brushing

500g onions, thinly sliced

1 tablespoon grated ginger

3 garlic cloves, finely grated

1 teaspoon chilli powder

1 teaspoon cumin seeds

1 teaspoon garam masala

350ml warm water

4 heaped tablespoons Greek yoghurt

75g melted butter

50g barberries or sour cherries

Large bunch of fresh coriander, finely chopped

700g fresh or frozen tilapia fillets (defrosted if frozen)

700g Maris Piper potatoes

Sea salt, to taste

Sweet, spiced caramelised onions with soft white tilapia fish, sour barberries and crunchy, crisp slices of golden potato… a total match made in heaven. This is a really fantastic centrepiece fish dish. If you can't get hold of tilapia, try using any white fish fillets or prawns instead.

Put the basmati rice in a sieve and rinse under the cold tap until the water runs clear. Bring a large pan of salted water to the boil, add the rinsed rice and cook for 5 minutes, then drain thoroughly and set aside.

Pour the olive oil into a frying pan, place over a low-medium heat and add the onions. Cook, stirring, for 20–25 minutes until they are a deep golden brown colour. Add the ginger, garlic, chilli powder, cumin seeds and garam masala and stir the whole mixture well to make sure the spices don't catch. Add 200ml of the warm water and the Greek yoghurt to the onions and cook for a further 10 minutes until you have a thick onion masala. Season generously with salt.

Preheat the oven to 200°C (180°C fan), gas mark 6. Mix the melted butter, barberries or sour cherries and chopped coriander together in a bowl. Take a wide, flat casserole dish and scatter the parboiled rice over the base. Spoon over the barberry-coriander butter and sprinkle over the remaining 150ml warm water. Next, place the tilapia fillets on top of the rice, followed by the onion masala.

Slice the potatoes as thinly as you can using a mandolin or sharp knife (there is no need to peel them as this adds to the final texture). Layer the potatoes over the top of the fish, brush them liberally with olive oil and season with sea salt. Transfer the casserole dish to the oven to cook, uncovered, for 20–30 minutes, or until the potatoes have crisped up.

NB *Tilapia is a beautiful meaty white fish. I often stock my freezer with frozen tilapia fillets – it is one of few fish that retains its texture after defrosting, and can take high cooking temperatures.*

Sticky Tamarind & Orange Salmon

SERVES 8

Olive oil, for greasing

1 whole skinless salmon fillet, about 1kg

8 tablespoons tamarind pulp

Juice of 4 oranges, plus zest of 1–2 oranges, to garnish

2 large red chillies, finely chopped

2 teaspoons ground cinnamon

2 teaspoon cumin seeds, dry-roasted and lightly crushed

4 heaped tablespoons honey

100g butter

100ml water

Large bunch of fresh coriander

Salt, to taste

This dish is a complete riot of colours, with soft, just-cooked pink salmon against the deep brown tamarind-orange sauce and emerald green flecks of coriander. You can use individual salmon fillets, but to feed a large crowd I like to cook a whole fillet, which everyone can share.

Grease a large baking tray with olive oil and place the salmon fillet in the centre.

Put the tamarind pulp, orange juice, red chillies, ground cinnamon, cumin seeds, honey, butter and measured water into a pan. Stir well to combine all the ingredients, then place over a low heat and simmer for about 5 minutes until the mixture has a saucy consistency. Season to taste with salt. Meanwhile, remove and finely chop the coriander stalks, reserving the leaves. Add the coriander stalks to the sauce and set aside to cool.

Preheat the oven to 200°C (180°C fan), gas mark 6.

Gently spoon the tamarind-orange sauce all over the salmon, making sure that all of the fish is completely covered. Transfer to the oven and bake for 12–14 minutes, or until the salmon is opaque all the way through (thicker fillets may need a couple more minutes).

Scatter the baked salmon with the fresh coriander leaves and orange zest and serve immediately.

Almond & Smoked Fish Koftas

with Watercress & Toasted Almond Salad

SERVES 4

400g Maris Piper potatoes, peeled and cut into chunks

25g butter

1 egg yolk

3 heaped tablespoons finely chopped fresh coriander

1 teaspoon finely diced red chilli

200g smoked haddock fillet

1 egg

75g flaked almonds

75g panko breadcrumbs

Spray oil

Salt, to taste

For the Salad

50ml olive oil

2 tablespoons sherry vinegar

½ red onion, thinly sliced

1 bag of watercress (about 100g)

50g flaked toasted almonds, toasted

Salt and black pepper, to taste

Although today almonds are used extensively in north Indian cuisine, it is thought that the Mughals popularised their use in Indian cookery in the sixteenth century. In south-east Asia, almonds are recommended in the winter months as they are believed to boost immunity and warm the blood and body. These koftas are a little like fishcakes – smooth, full-bodied potato, smoky, soft-fleshed fish and the satisfying crunch of sweet buttery almonds.

Boil the potatoes in a large pan of salted water. When the potatoes are cooked through, drain them in a colander and leave them for 15 minutes to steam dry. Mash the potatoes using a ricer or potato masher until they are very smooth. Add the butter, egg yolk, chopped coriander and chilli to the mashed potato and combine well with a wooden spoon. Season to taste with salt.

Put the smoked haddock in a shallow pan and cover with warm water. Place over a low heat and poach the fish gently for about 5 minutes, or until the fish starts flaking. Remove the fish from the poaching liquid and allow cool slightly before flaking it into the mashed potatoes. You want to be careful at this point to not overmix the fish, as it is much nicer to have larger pieces running through the kofta. Cover the bowl with cling film and transfer to the fridge for about 30–60 minutes. This resting time is essential, as it will allow the potato mix to firm up.

When you are ready to cook, preheat the oven to 220°C (200°C fan), gas mark 7 and line a baking tray with baking parchment. Beat the egg in a shallow bowl. Crunch the flaked almonds in your hands to break them up into slightly smaller pieces. Mix the almonds with the panko breadcrumbs and place them on a tray.

A processional scene, as depicted on the walls of the Juna Mahal in Dungarpur, India.

Using lightly oiled hands, shape the potato kofta mixture into small rounds, about the size of a walnut. Dip the koftas into the beaten egg, followed by the almond crumb mixture. Place the koftas onto the lined baking tray and spray all over with oil. Bake for 20–25 minutes, or until the koftas are golden and crisp.

Meanwhile, assemble the salad. Whisk together the olive oil and vinegar and season with salt and pepper. Drop the onion into the vinaigrette and allow to steep for 15 minutes. Put the watercress into a serving bowl and pour over the steeped onion slices and vinaigrette; mix well so that each piece of watercress is coated. Scatter over the toasted flaked almonds and serve with the hot fish koftas.

Sea Bass, Chilli & Saffron Butter

Baked in Lavash

SERVES 4

4 pieces of lavash bread
Good pinch of saffron threads
1 garlic clove, finely grated
1 red chilli, finely chopped
50g softened butter
4 x 120g skinless sea bass fillets, about 1cm thick
2 sliced spring onions, thinly sliced
Handful of fresh coriander
Olive oil
Salt, to taste

Lavash is an incredibly versatile Persian flatbread that is usually used to make light wraps and rolls. I wrap fillets of sea bass in it and roast the bread parcels until they are golden on the outside and crunchy in texture. This is a really quick and easy supper for the family or guests.

Preheat the oven to 200°C (180°C fan), gas mark 6.

Trim each piece of lavash bread to create four squares around 20 x 20cm. Use a fork to mix the saffron, garlic and red chilli into the softened butter.

Season the sea bass fillets with salt and place each one onto a square of lavash bread. Spread the saffron-chilli butter over the sea bass fillets and sprinkle with a few spring onions and some coriander. Carefully bring each side of the lavash over the sea bass so that the fish is completely enclosed inside the flatbread.

Place the prepared fish parcels onto a baking tray and rub olive oil all over them. Bake for about 12 minutes, or until the fish is cooked through and the bread is golden. Open out the fish parcel to reveal the herb and saffron baked fish and crispy lavash bread. Serve immediately.

Swordfish Steaks
with Tomato, Ginger & Fenugreek Sauce

SERVES 4

4 tablespoons olive oil, plus extra for rubbing

2 red onions, thinly sliced

1½ teaspoons grated ginger

1 garlic clove, finely grated

1 tablespoon dried fenugreek leaves

½ teaspoon ground turmeric

1 teaspoon ground cumin

1 teaspoon ground coriander

750g cherry tomatoes

1 green chilli

100g fresh fenugreek, leaves picked

1 teaspoon sugar

4 x 150–175g swordfish steaks, about 2cm thick

Salt, to taste

The Mughal emperors were forever consulting with their physicians when it came to planning their meals. Food was eaten for pleasure, but the medicinal property of ingredients was of utmost importance. The use of the fenugreek plant in the region occupied by the Mughal Empire is well documented; the plant has been used as a remedy for asthma and arthritis, to improve digestion, maintain metabolism and even as a cure for sore throats. The plant produces aromatic brown seeds but the leaves, known as *methi*, are commonly used in Pakistani, north Indian and Kashmiri recipes. The leaves can be used in both the dried and fresh forms, and impart a rich, herbal, earthy and mellow note to curries. Chicken and lamb take particularly well to its complex flavour, but swordfish is a wonderful full-bodied fish alternative. Fenugreek leaves are now readily available in UK supermarkets.

Pour the olive oil into a pan and place over a low-medium heat. Add the onions and cook for 20 minutes until they are golden brown in colour. Add the ginger, garlic, dried fenugreek leaves, turmeric, cumin and coriander and fry the spices briefly to release their aromas.

Put the cherry tomatoes and green chilli into a food processor or blender and blitz to form a purée. Add this tomato purée to the onion mixture and cook over a low heat for about 15 minutes until well reduced.

Stir the fresh fenugreek leaves into the tomato sauce and simmer for 5 minutes until the fenugreek leaves have wilted. If the sauce is looking too thick, loosen with a few tablespoons of water. Season the sauce with salt and a teaspoon of sugar to counter the acidity of the tomatoes.

Rub the swordfish steaks with a little olive oil and sprinkle with salt. Place a griddle pan over a high heat and add the swordfish steaks. Cook for 2–3 minutes each side, or until the steaks have just cooked through, and the griddle marks are visible. Lay the steaks over the tomato and fenugreek sauce and serve.

Mughal Baked Cod Korma

SERVES 4

75ml olive oil

2 onions, sliced

1 garlic clove, finely grated

1 teaspoon grated ginger

1 teaspoon garam masala

1 red chilli (medium strength), finely diced

½ teaspoon ground turmeric

1 teaspoon ground coriander

1 teaspoon cumin seeds

50g whole almonds

250ml warm water

Good pinch of saffron threads, soaked in a few tablespoons of warm water

2 heaped tablespoons Greek yoghurt

4 x 200g cod fillets

Handful of flaked almonds

Salt, to taste

Almonds were used extensively in Mughal cuisine; they were revered for their flavour as well as their ability to provide a thick, buttery texture to dishes. The korma is rumoured to have developed in Hyderabad, a city whose food heritage is heavily influenced by the Mughal Empire. The traditional korma is creamy, nutty and gently spiced, quite unlike many of the versions of korma made today.

Preheat the oven to 220°C (200°C fan), gas mark 7 and lightly oil a roasting tin.

Heat the olive oil in a pan, add the onions and fry over a low-medium heat for 15–20 minutes until they are soft and golden brown. Add the garlic, ginger, garam masala, red chilli, turmeric, ground coriander and cumin seeds and fry lightly to allow the spices to release their aroma; take care not to let the spices to catch.

Remove the spiced onions from the heat and allow to cool slightly. Tip into a food processor or blender with the whole almonds and measured warm water. Blitz to a very smooth purée and then transfer to a pan, season with salt and cook over a medium heat for 5–10 minutes to reduce the mixture down to a thick, saucy consistency. Remove from the heat and allow to cool.

Use a fork to whisk the saffron and its soaking liquid into the yoghurt. Now gently combine the saffron yoghurt into the almond sauce and set aside.

Place the fish in the roasting tray and spoon over the prepared korma sauce. Sprinkle over the flaked almonds and bake for 12 minutes until the fish is just cooked through. Serve with boiled rice and any green salad of your choice.

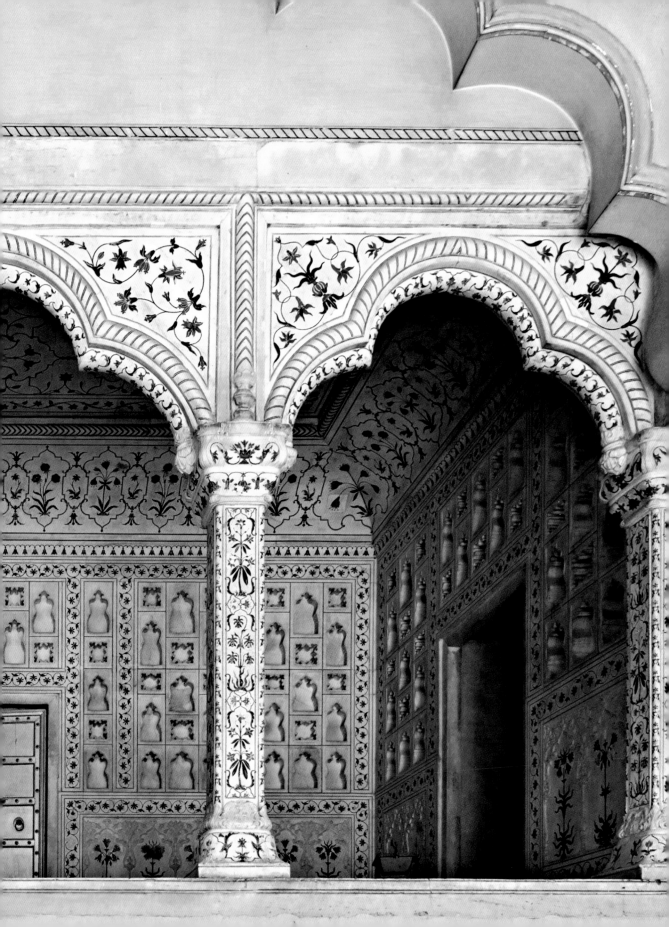

with Spiced Yoghurt Dipping Sauce
Fiery King Prawns

SERVES 4

1 heaped teaspoon hot paprika

1–2 red chillies, finely chopped

1 teaspoon mustard seeds

1 tablespoon honey

1 teaspoon grated ginger

75ml melted butter

Juice of 1 lime

600g large raw prawns, shelled and deveined

Salt, to taste

For the Yoghurt Sauce

300ml natural yoghurt, at room temperature

60ml olive oil

½ teaspoon mustard seeds

½ teaspoon cumin seeds

½ teaspoon chilli flakes

¼ teaspoon ground turmeric

Pinch of paprika

Salt, to taste

As a teenager, I attended a family wedding in the city of Karachi, Pakistan, a bustling, cosmopolitan port city, and my senses were overloaded in every way possible. At the wedding celebration I remember being served gigantic skewers loaded with plump juicy prawns that had been cooked in the tandoor oven. They were feverishly smoky, subtly spiced, sea sweet and utterly, utterly delicious. I have recreated that memory here – you can cook these under the grill, in a griddle pan or on the barbecue in the summer. I like to keep the tails on the prawns when I shell them as it looks rather attractive.

Mix the paprika, chillies, mustard seeds, honey, ginger, melted butter and lime juice together in a large bowl. Add the prawns and season to taste with salt. Massage the marinade into the prawns; if possible allow them to marinate for 15–20 minutes.

Pour the yoghurt into a bowl and season to taste with salt. Heat the olive oil in a small pan over a high heat; when it is very hot, add the mustard seeds, cumin seeds, chilli flakes and turmeric. As soon as the spices start popping, carefully pour the searing hot oil onto the yoghurt. Swirl the spiced oil into the yoghurt to create a marbled effect but be careful as the fat will spit a bit when you do this. Dust with a pinch of paprika.

Preheat the grill to high or place a griddle pan or non-stick frying pan over a high heat. Cook the prawns for a couple of minutes each side, turning them only once during cooking. They should end up with a nice charred tinge to them. Serve immediately, with the spiced yoghurt.

Lentils & Vegetables

Emperor Akbar, a great patron of the arts, was deeply fond of vegetarian cookery. His highness bought horticulturalists from Persia to improve the quality of existing produce, and help the cultivation of new varieties of vegetables. There are even records of the vegetables in the imperial kitchen gardens being nourished with rose water so that they would smell fragrant when cooked.

Akbar was so fond of vegetarian cooking that records suggest that with the passage of time he began to eat meat less and less. He first abstained from eating meat on Fridays, then Sundays, then the first of each month, and finally the whole month of March and October. His fondness for vegetables was relished by the Hindu cooks in the vegetarian section of the imperial kitchen who produced an array of highly innovative dishes to please and delight the emperor. Vegetarian food was also given its own name, the so-called *sufiyana* cookery of the Mughal era.

Digging deeper, it seems that even the most carnivorous of Mughal emperors had their favoured vegetable dishes; Emperor Aurangzeb was a committed vegetarian for much of his life. The vegetarian dishes in this chapter draw influence from far and wide and will certainly not leave anyone craving meat.

Courgettes

Stuffed with Chana Dal & Tamarind

SERVES 4

4 large or 8 small courgettes

175g chana dal (yellow split lentils), ideally soaked in warm water for 1 hour

1 tablespoon olive oil, plus extra for drizzling

1 teaspoon cumin seeds

½ teaspoon ground turmeric

1 teaspoon garam masala

1 tablespoon tomato purée

2 tablespoons tamarind pulp

250ml warm water

1 teaspoon chilli flakes

Juice of ½ lemon

Handful of chopped fresh coriander, plus extra to garnish

Salt, to taste

2 tablespoons sour cream or yoghurt, to serve

Stuffed vegetables in their numerous forms have always been a personal favourite of mine. My grandmother used to stuff chana dal into bitter gourds in the winter months, tie them with string and steam them gently in a spiced tomato sauce – this dish is in memory of her. There is something so deeply satisfying about cutting into these soft courgettes, revealing the decadent spiced lentil stuffing. A beautifully rustic, family-friendly dish.

———————————————

Cut the courgettes in half lengthways. Use the handle of a teaspoon to carefully scoop out the centre of the courgettes, take care to keep the 'shells' intact.

Drain the soaked chana dal and add to a large pan of boiling water. Cook for about 30 minutes – the lentils should keep their shape but will break up when pressed between your fingers. Drain the cooked chana dal and set aside.

Pour the olive oil into a pan, place over a medium heat and add the cumin seeds. Allow them to sizzle and release their aroma, then add the turmeric, parboiled chana dal, garam masala, tomato purée, tamarind and measured warm water to bring everything together. Sprinkle in the chilli flakes, lemon juice and chopped coriander and season to taste with salt. Set aside to cool while you preheat the oven to 200°C (180°C fan), gas mark 6.

Carefully stuff the courgettes with the cooled lentils, then put them into a deep roasting tin and drizzle with a little more olive oil. Bake covered for 20 minutes and then uncovered for a further 15 minutes, until the courgettes have cooked through. Serve warm, drizzled with sour cream or yoghurt and garnished with chopped coriander.

Smoky Spiced Aubergine & Pomegranate
Vol-au-vents

2 large aubergines (about 800g total weight)

2 tablespoons olive oil, plus extra for drizzling

1 onion, thinly sliced

1 teaspoon hot paprika

½ teaspoon chilli powder

1 heaped teaspoon cumin seeds, dry-roasted

1 heaped tablespoon pomegranate molasses

1 x 320g sheet of puff pastry

Flour, for dusting

1 beaten egg

3 tablespoons sour cream

Handful of pomegranate seeds

Handful of chopped fresh flat-leaf parsley

20g toasted pistachios

Salt, to taste

My relationship with aubergines is nothing short of a full-blown love affair. They are a complete textural delight and are the most incredible sponge for flavour. I adore this dish – it makes an incredible vegetarian main course or starter. The combination of aubergine, sweet pomegranate molasses and chilli heat is so pleasing against the flaky butter-enriched puff pastry.

Preheat the oven to 200°C (180°C fan), gas mark 6.

Cut the aubergines in half lengthways, drizzle with a small amount of olive oil and bake for about 30 minutes, or until the aubergine has softened completely. Allow the aubergines to cool, scoop out the flesh and put to one side.

Add the 2 tablespoons of olive oil to a pan, place over a medium heat and add the onion. Fry the onion for 15–20 minutes until it turns a deep golden brown, then add the paprika, chilli powder and cumin seeds. Cook gently for 1 minute until the spices release their aroma. Add the aubergine flesh to the pan along with the pomegranate molasses and mix thoroughly. Cook the mixture for a few minutes until the oil starts rising to the surface of the aubergines. Season to taste with salt and allow the mixture to cool.

To make the vol-au-vent cases, remove the pastry from the fridge and unroll onto a lightly floured worktop. Working quickly while the pastry is still cool, cut it into four 8cm squares. Carefully place the pastry squares onto a baking tray lined with baking parchment. Use a knife to score a shallow border about 1.5cm from the edge, taking care to not cut the whole way through. Prick the inner part with a fork and brush the border with the beaten egg. Chill in the fridge for at least 30 minutes.

Increase the oven temperature to 220°C (200°C fan), gas mark 6 and bake the vol-au-vents for 12–15 minutes, or until the pastry is golden and puffed up. Remove from the oven and allow the vol-au-vents to cool.

Scoop out the top layer of the pastry from the centre of the vol-au-vents to create a 'nest' and fill the vol-au-vents with the aubergine mixture. Dollop over the sour cream and scatter with the pomegranate seeds, chopped parsley and toasted pistachios. Serve immediately.

Whole Roast Cauliflower

SERVES 4

1 small cauliflower (about 600g)
1 teaspoon ground turmeric
1 teaspoon melted butter
1 tablespoon olive oil
1 garlic clove, finely grated
1 teaspoon grated ginger
Good pinch of saffron threads
1 teaspoon cumin seeds
1 teaspoon hot paprika
1 teaspoon black mustard seeds
1 red chilli (medium strength), thinly sliced
1 teaspoon sugar
1 x 400ml tin full-fat coconut milk
Handful of toasted cashews
Handful of fresh coriander leaves
Salt, to taste

This is one of the most impressive vegetarian centrepiece dishes. The golden baked cauliflower globes have the perfect texture; not too mushy and not too crunchy. The coconut milk, cashews and saffron give the dish a sensational, deep, earthy flavour.

Remove the outer leaves of the cauliflower and trim the base so that the cauliflower can stand upright. Bring a large pan of water to the boil and add the turmeric, mixing well to create a deep yellow-coloured broth. Place the cauliflower upside down into the turmeric water and boil for 4 minutes. Drain in a colander and allow the cauliflower to steam dry for about 30 minutes.

Preheat the oven to 200°C (180°C fan), gas mark 6.

Whisk together the melted butter, olive oil, garlic, ginger, saffron, cumin seeds, paprika, black mustard seeds, sliced chilli and sugar in a small bowl. Pour this mixture over the cauliflower, rubbing it into all the cracks and crevices. Sprinkle salt over the cauliflower.

Pour the coconut milk into the base of a small roasting tin (about 20cm square) and place the cauliflower on top. Roast for about 30 minutes, basting the cauliflower with the coconut milk after 15 minutes. The surface of the cauliflower should be charred and deep golden, with a thick coconut milk sauce at the bottom of the tin. If it hasn't reduced down, transfer the juices to a saucepan and reduce down to form a sauce-like consistency. Sprinkle over the toasted cashews and coriander and serve immediately, either as the centrepiece dish or as part of a spread.

with Mint & Sour Cream
Beetroot Curry

1kg raw beetroot

75ml vegetable oil

2 onions, cut into 2cm chunks

6 garlic cloves, finely grated

1 teaspoon grated ginger

½ teaspoon ground turmeric

1 teaspoon nigella seeds

1 teaspoon cumin seeds

1 green chilli, finely chopped

½ teaspoon chilli powder

3 ripe tomatoes, cut into large chunks

500ml warm water

75g sour cream

Zest of 1 lemon

Handful of fresh mint leaves, thinly sliced

Salt, to taste

The traditional way of eating beetroot in Pakistan is as part of a rich, spicy lamb curry. And while my carnivorous side loves cooking lamb with beets, there is no denying the alluring simplicity of how the ruby rich beetroot is treated in this dish. Perfect with lashings of sour cream and a flatbread of your choice.

Wearing plastic gloves to prevent your hands becoming stained, peel the beetroot and cut them in half lengthways. Now slice each beetroot half into semicircles about 1cm thick and set aside.

Pour the vegetable oil into a pan and place over a medium heat. Add the onions and fry for 3–4 minutes. Once the onions start becoming translucent and soft, add the garlic, ginger, turmeric, nigella and cumin seeds, green chilli and chilli powder and stir well to make sure that the spices don't catch. Add the chopped tomatoes and half the measured warm water and cook, stirring, for about 10 minutes until the sauce has reduced down, oil rises to the surface and the tomatoes start breaking down.

Add the beetroot slices to the pan and mix well, ensuring that each piece of beetroot is coated in the sauce. Add the remaining warm water and simmer over a low heat for 30–40 minutes, or until the beetroot is cooked through but still holding its shape (top up with a little more warm water if pan starts to look dry).

Before serving season to taste with salt, drizzle over the sour cream and scatter with the lemon zest and sliced mint leaves.

Saag & Cornmeal Bread

SERVES 4

50g mustard leaves (or use spinach), chopped

75ml ghee (see Note)

6 garlic cloves, thinly sliced

1 teaspoon chilli flakes

2 tablespoons natural yoghurt

1 tablespoon chopped fresh coriander

Salt, to taste

For the Cornmeal Bread

200g fine cornmeal (maize flour)

100g chapatti flour, plus extra for dusting

1 tablespoon dried fenugreek leaves

1 teaspoon nigella seeds

½ teaspoon chilli powder

1 tablespoon ghee, plus extra for brushing

Salt, to taste

NB *If you can't get hold of ghee, use unsalted butter instead.*

Sources suggest that Emperor Akbar had a particular love for a lightly spiced spinach dish called saag. Saag (which actually translates as 'greens') remains an extremely popular dish in the Punjab today, where in its simplest form it is enjoyed in quaint little villages with cornmeal bread. There is something so pure and unadulterated about this dish; its rustic flavours give it the most unique appeal.

Bring a large pan of water to the boil and drop the mustard leaves into the pan. Cook for 12–15 minutes until the stalks of the mustard leaves have softened (if you are using spinach, cook the leaves for just a couple of minutes). Drain the mustard leaves in a colander and set aside.

Put the ghee into a pan and place over a medium heat. When it is warm, add the garlic and fry until it starts turning golden brown. Add the drained cooked mustard leaves and stir the whole mixture really well. Add the chilli flakes and season to taste with salt. Use a potato masher to break down some of the mustard leaves in the pan: the final texture should be that of a coarse purée. Finish by adding the yoghurt and fresh coriander.

To make the cornmeal bread, add the cornmeal and chapatti flour to a bowl together with the fenugreek leaves, nigella seeds, chilli powder and salt to taste. Pour in the ghee and just enough water to bring the mixture together with your hands to form a soft dough. Divide the dough into eight equal-sized balls.

Dust the worktop with some chapatti flour. Roll each dough ball into a circle about 15cm in diameter and about 2–3mm thick. Place a non-stick frying pan over a medium heat and cook the flatbreads for 2–3 minutes on each side until they are golden coloured and cooked through (they will be quite crumbly in texture). Brush with ghee before serving with the saag.

Sour & Spicy Pink Radishes

SERVES 2

2 tablespoons vegetable oil
½ red onion, finely diced
1 tablespoon grated ginger
½ teaspoon cumin seeds
1 red chilli, thinly sliced
350g pink radishes, quartered
2–3 tablespoons tamarind pulp
Handful of fresh coriander leaves
Salt, to taste

As a child visiting my grandmother's home in Pakistan, I remember sprinkling salt over radishes and munching on them at lunchtime. Over the years I have experimented with radishes and found them to be an incredibly versatile ingredient – I stir-fry them, braise them in stews, pickle them and eat them raw in salads. In this dish, which works as a side dish or snack, the peppery fire of the radish complements the tart tamarind while the fresh citrus of coriander lifts the dish to new heights.

Pour the oil into a wok and place over a high heat. When it is hot, add the diced onion and fry until it just starts turning golden, about 3–5 minutes. Next add the ginger, cumin seeds and red chilli and mix well, allowing the spices to release their aromas.

Drop the quartered radishes into the wok and cook for about 5 minutes over a high heat. Finally add the tamarind and mix well. Add a handful of fresh chopped coriander leaves, season with salt to taste and serve immediately, with flatbreads or scattered over some salad leaves.

 NB You may wish to use large white Daikon radishes instead of pink ones – in which case, slice the radishes into 1cm-thick semicircles and prepare as described above.

Watermelon Curry

SERVES 4–6

100g seedless watermelon, cubed

100ml olive oil

2 onions, finely diced

1 teaspoon grated ginger

1 teaspoon black mustard seeds

½ teaspoon ground turmeric

½ teaspoon chilli powder

½ teaspoon garam masala

2 x 400g tins chickpeas, rinsed and drained

Handful of chopped fresh coriander, to garnish

Salt, to taste

When Emperor Babur moved from the temperate climates of Afghanistan and central Asia to India, he longed for melon. There are accounts of him weeping when an imported watermelon was cut open in front of him. 'How can one forget the pleasures of those lands?' he proclaimed.

Today in India, the province of Rajasthan celebrates the watermelon by making the most delicious and light watermelon curry. I am really very excited to share this well-kept secret with you.

Set a small handful of watermelon cubes to one side for the garnish and put the remainder into a food processor or blender. Blitz to a smooth purée and set aside.

Pour the olive oil into a pan, place over a medium heat and add the onions. When they have softened and started turning golden, after about 15 minutes, add the ginger, mustard seeds, turmeric, chilli powder and garam masala and stir vigorously to ensure that the spices don't catch.

Add the chickpeas and combine all the ingredients well, then cook for 5 minutes before adding the watermelon purée. Allow the whole mixture to simmer gently for 25–30 minutes, then season to taste with salt.

Just before serving, drop the reserved cubed watermelon into the curry along with the coriander. Serve with boiled white rice.

Creamy Mung Dal
with Cumin Butter & Sourdough Toast

SERVES 4

300g moong/mung dal (huskless split mung beans)

2 litres water

½ teaspoon ground turmeric

6 garlic cloves, thinly sliced

¾ teaspoon chilli powder (less if you prefer it mild)

1 bay leaf

4 tablespoons ghee, plus extra for the bread

1 onion, thinly sliced

1 teaspoon cumin seeds, dry-roasted and lightly crushed

1 teaspoon softened butter

4–8 slices of sourdough bread

Salt, to taste

Handful of fresh coriander leaves, to garnish

This dish has the magical ability to please, whether enjoyed on long summer days, cold winter nights, lazy autumn afternoons or at sunsets in early spring. It will envelope you in a comforting embrace and make life that little bit better!

Wash the mung dal in a sieve under cold running water until the water runs clear, then add to a large pan with the measured water. Bring to the boil and add the turmeric, garlic, chilli powder and bay leaf. (Don't season with salt at this stage as it can make the lentils tough.) Lower the heat and allow the mixture to simmer for about 1½ hours, or until the lentils have broken down and become creamy and smooth. You may occasionally need to spoon off any scum that rises to the surface. Check that the lentils are not drying up, topping up with warm water if needed. The lentils will need to be stirred frequently in the last 30 minutes of their cooking – this will help them break down into a smooth texture.

Melt the ghee in a small frying pan over a medium heat, and add the sliced onion and fry for 20–25 minutes. When it is a deep golden brown colour, add it to the lentils and season to taste with salt.

Add the toasted crushed cumin seeds to the softened butter, mix well and transfer to the fridge to firm up while you preheat the oven to 200°C (180°C fan), gas mark 6.

Rub a small amount of ghee over the sourdough slices, arrange them on a baking tray and bake and for 5–7 minutes until the sourdough slices are golden and crisp.

Serve the mung dal piping hot in deep bowls with a sprinkling of fresh coriander, a knob of the cumin butter and the crisp sourdough on the side.

Roasted Grapes
& Homemade Paneer Cheese

SERVES 2

2.5 litres whole milk

4 tablespoons malt vinegar

20 purple grapes

2 tablespoons honey

2 tablespoons olive oil

½ teaspoon chilli flakes

½ teaspoon cumin seeds, coarsely crushed

4 brined vine leaves

Salt, to taste

The Mughals took a keen interest in horticulture, and viticulture, which is the horticulture of grapes, was a particular speciality. To this day there are Mughal grape gardens in northern Pakistan, where the wet weather and fertile soil are perfect for the cultivation of huge clusters of plump, violet-skinned grapes. In this dish, the pairing of milky paneer against the sweet grapes is really quite special.

Pour the milk into a large pan and bring to the boil. Add the malt vinegar to the milk – you will see the milk curdling within a minute or so. If the milk does not curdle, add a little more vinegar. As soon as the milk curdles, remove from the heat and strain it through a sieve lined with a muslin cloth or large clean J-cloth to separate the curds and whey. It is important that the curdled milk does not spend too much time on the hob as the curds will harden otherwise. Discard the whey and gently rinse the curds in warm water to get rid of the flavour of vinegar. Season the curds with salt and transfer to a clean muslin cloth. Bring up the four corners and tie them together, then suspend the 'parcel' over a bowl or the sink for at least an hour – a good tip is to attach it to your kitchen tap.

Meanwhile, put the grapes into a bowl with the honey, olive oil, chilli flakes, cumin seeds and salt to taste and stir to combine. Preheat the oven to 200°C (180°C fan), gas mark 6.

Lay the vine leaves out on your worktop so that they are slightly overlapping each other to make a large square or circle. Carefully remove the paneer cheese from the muslin cloth and place it in the middle of the vine leaves. Bring the edges of the leaves over the paneer to loosely wrap it (don't worry if the central portion is exposed). Place the vine-wrapped paneer into a small roasting tin or ovenproof dish and scatter the grapes around it. Bake for 8–12 minutes, or until the grapes are beautifully sticky and caramelised and the paneer has just warmed through. Serve immediately while the grapes and milky paneer are still warm.

'Patta Gobi' Spiced Cabbage

SERVES 2

75ml olive oil
½ teaspoon mustard seeds
1 teaspoon grated ginger
½ teaspoon ground turmeric
1 green chilli, thinly sliced
500g cabbage, shredded
1 teaspoon sugar
70g fresh fenugreek, leaves picked
Salt, to taste

When the British arrived in India in the eighteenth century, towards the end of the Mughal Empire, it is thought that along with potatoes, carrots and peas, they brought with them the humble cabbage. In India, cabbage (*patta gobi*) was of course treated in many new and innovative ways. This recipe is a fine example of how a handful of simple spices can completely transform a vegetable.

_____

Pour the olive oil into a wok and place over a high heat. When the oil is very hot add the mustard seeds, ginger, turmeric and green chilli. When the mustard seeds are popping vigorously, quickly add the shredded cabbage. Stir well so that the cabbage takes on the pale-yellow hue of the turmeric.

Add the sugar and season to taste with salt. The cabbage will take about 5 minutes to cook through in the wok – it should be wilted and slightly soft, but still retain some bite.

To finish the dish, add the fenugreek leaves and cook, stirring, for a final minute. Serve immediately.

Mountain Mushrooms

SERVES 2

Olive oil, for frying

450g mixed mushrooms, such as chestnut and Portobello, roughly chopped

2 tablespoons honey

8g walnuts, plus a few to garnish

20g sesame seeds, plus a few to garnish

1 teaspoon cumin seeds

1 teaspoon chilli flakes

1 red onion, thinly sliced

1 garlic clove, finely grated

1 teaspoon grated ginger

¼ teaspoon ground turmeric

Salt, to taste

For the Mughal emperors, vegetarian dishes were no simple fare. Vegetables were treated with the utmost care and attention, the result being a delectable array of vegetable curries. Both mushrooms and walnuts are particularly abundant in the mountainous region of Kashmir, and this earthy, smoky, nutty combination of flavours is a definite crowd pleaser.

Drizzle a few tablespoons of olive oil into a large frying pan and heat until the oil is practically smoking. Add the mushrooms and fry for a few minutes until they are cooked through and are starting to turn golden. Drizzle in the honey and season with plenty of salt. Once the mushrooms are golden and sticky, take them off the heat and set aside.

Place a separate dry frying pan over a medium heat and toast the walnuts, sesame seeds and cumin seeds one by one, tipping the toasted ingredients into a food processor or blender once they become golden. Add the chilli flakes and blitz to form a slightly coarse nutty powder. Be careful not to over-blitz this mixture or the walnuts will start releasing their oils and the final dish will lack texture.

Take another large non-stick frying pan and fry the onion in a few tablespoons of olive oil over a high heat until it starts to turn golden, about 5 minutes. Stir in the garlic, ginger and turmeric followed by the blitzed walnut/sesame/spice mixture and stir well to prevent the mixture from sticking.

Finally, add the honey-glazed mushrooms to the walnuts and onions and mix thoroughly and quickly – do not keep the mushrooms in the pan for longer than a few minutes as they will overcook and the walnuts will start catching. Serve with a scattering of extra chopped toasted walnuts and sesame seeds, as an accompaniment to meat dishes or with flatbreads.

Mughal Eggs & Beans

75ml vegetable oil, plus extra for drizzling

2 onions, finely diced

1 garlic clove, finely grated

1 teaspoon hot paprika

1 teaspoon chilli flakes, plus a pinch for sprinkling

1 teaspoon ground coriander

½ teaspoon ground turmeric

Pinch of asafoetida

Handful of curry leaves (fresh or frozen)

2 x 400g tins haricot beans, rinsed and drained

1 tablespoon tomato purée

250ml warm water

2–3 tablespoons maple syrup

1 tablespoon tamarind pulp

2 tablespoons crème fraîche

2 eggs

Salt, to taste

Handful of chopped fresh coriander, to garnish

There are many historical accounts that tell us that eggs were a favoured ingredient in the Mughal Court where they were cooked either on their own or combined with pulses, vegetables and meat. This wholesome vegetarian dish is full of protein. It is a family favourite, which we enjoy at brunch on weekends.

Pour the oil into a large, lidded frying pan, place over a medium heat and add the onions. Fry the onions, stirring, for about 15 minutes until they are uniformly deep golden brown. Add the garlic, paprika, chilli flakes, coriander, turmeric, asafoetida and curry leaves and stir the mixture well to release the aroma from the spices.

Add the drained haricot beans and tomato purée and stir well to combine all the ingredients in the pan. Add the measured warm water, maple syrup and tamarind along with a healthy pinch of salt. Taste the beans and adjust any seasonings to your taste. Turn the heat down low and allow the beans to simmer for about 15 minutes, or until they have a saucy texture.

Make two hollows in the beans with the back of your spoon. Spoon the crème fraîche into the hollows and gently crack the eggs over the crème fraîche. Place a lid over the beans and simmer very gently for a further 8–10 minutes, or until the eggs have cooked through. If you overheat at this stage, the eggs will be rubbery and the beans may reduce down too much, so keep the heat really low to stop this happening. Garnish the eggs and beans with a sprinkle of chilli flakes, the chopped coriander and a drizzle of olive oil.

 NB You can use any tinned beans of your choice – red kidney, black-eyed peas or borlotti beans are good alternatives.

Rice
& Bread

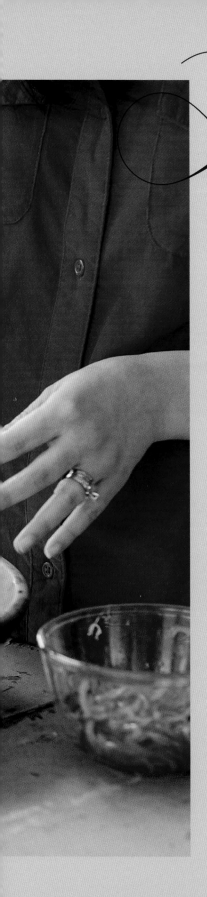

Jean-Baptiste Tavernier, the seventeenth-century French traveller, remarked, 'When you wish to make an acceptable present to anyone in Persia, you take him a sack of rice'.

The Persians certainly did excel in the creation of the most sublime rice dishes: variations included fruit, nuts, turmeric and saffron. Rice was treated carefully, so that the grains swelled without clumping and the delicate aroma of cooked rice wafted in the air.

Mumtaz Mahal was Emperor Shah Jahan's wife. When Mumtaz passed away in 1631, Shah Jahan was completely grief-stricken. It is said that in his despair he even 'gave up the practice of plucking out grey hair from his beard'. In the most grandiose gesture to lost love, Shah Jahan built the Taj Mahal as a memorial to his late wife.

Legend dictates that in her life, Mumtaz Mahal once visited the Mughal army barracks and found soldiers looking extremely weak and malnourished. This concerned Mumtaz and the biryani was allegedly first created on her orders in an attempt to plump up soldiers fighting for the empire.

Whether there is truth in this legend or not, we can all agree that the biryani is undoubtedly one of the culinary wonders of the world. The use of Persian methods for cooking rice and the addition of novel ingredients such as ginger, pepper, chilli and cloves have created the most sumptuous rice dish imaginable, of which there are now thousands of variations.

In Mughal times bread was made by bakers in the *rikab khanah*, or bakery. There were breads called bazurg tanuri that were baked in the oven with raising agents; in contrast, flatbreads called tanak tabqi were made on flat metal plates. This chapter of *Khazana* has a selection of raised and flatbreads inspired by the Mughal art of bread making.

Jewelled Persian Rice

350g basmati rice, soaked in water for at least 1 hour

1 cinnamon stick

5 cloves

5 cardamom pods

1 star anise

100g butter

Good pinch of saffron threads

1 carrot, cut into julienne

1 teaspoon sugar

50g pine nuts, dry-roasted

50g slivered pistachios

50g raisins

30g barberries

75g dried apricots, chopped

1 tablespoon rose water

75ml warm milk

To Garnish (optional)

1 tablespoon vegetable oil

1 onion, thinly sliced

The Mughals were connoisseurs of jewellery making as well as food. It is therefore fitting that this colourful rice dish is called jawahar pulao, or jewelled rice. The exotic saffron-flavoured basmati rice layered with slivered pistachios, pine nuts, raisins, apricots, barberries and julienned carrots is truly a feast for the eyes and senses. A particularly special accompaniment to any meat-based curry, kebab or fish dish.

_____

Preheat the oven to 200°C (180°C fan), gas mark 6.

Drain the soaked rice and rinse thoroughly under the cold tap until the water runs clear. Bring a large pan of salted water to the boil and add the drained rice, along with the cinnamon stick, cloves, cardamom pods and star anise. After exactly 6 minutes, drain the rice in a colander and set aside. Remove and discard the whole spices.

Melt the butter in a small pan, add the saffron and set aside to steep for at least 30 minutes, so that the saffron releases all of its flavour and colour into the butter.

Put a tablespoon of the saffron butter into a frying pan, add the carrot julienne and sugar and sauté over a medium heat for a couple of minutes. Once the carrots have softened, take them off the heat and put them into a bowl.

Add another tablespoon of saffron butter to the same pan and fry the pine nuts, pistachios, raisins and barberries for 2–3 minutes, then tip into the same bowl as the carrots, stirring to combine.

Spoon the parboiled rice into a casserole dish. Scatter over the chopped apricots, carrots and fried fruit and nuts, stirring gently with a fork to combine. Pour the remaining saffron butter over the rice and splash over the rose water and milk. Place a lid on the casserole dish and bake in the oven for 25–30 minutes.

While the rice is in the oven, prepare the garnish, if using. Heat the oil in a small frying pan and add the onion slices. Fry over a medium heat for about 20 minutes, stirring occasionally, until the onion is caramelised and dark brown. Drain on kitchen paper.

Garnish the rice with the caramelised onion and serve immediately.

Chickpea & Lamb Chop Polow

SERVES 4–6

125g butter

1 tablespoon olive oil

2 onions, thinly sliced

8–12 lamb chops, trimmed of excess fat

8 garlic cloves, finely grated

1 tablespoon grated ginger

1 litre warm water

2 bay leaves

1 small cinnamon stick

2 teaspoons garam masala

500g basmati rice, soaked in water for at least 1 hour

1 x 400g tin chickpeas, rinsed and drained

Salt, to taste

The fragrance of spiced rice and lamb wafting from the kitchen when this polow cooks is unparalleled. It instantly reminds me of my childhood, my heritage and celebrations. For me this is the definition of comfort food.

Each family has their own way of cooking polow and this recipe has been gifted to me by my mother-in-law. The key is the onions: you have to make sure you give them time to caramelise and become a deep shade of brown, as this will ultimately give a beautiful brown hue to the finished dish.

Melt the butter in a large, heavy-based casserole dish and add the oil and onions. Fry the onions over a medium heat for 20–25 minutes until they are a deep dark brown colour but not burned in any way. Add the lamb chops, garlic and ginger along with 250ml of the measured warm water to prevent the mixture from sticking and to prevent the onions from browning any further. Cook the lamb chops in the onions for about 15 minutes, stirring constantly.

Pour the remaining warm water into the casserole dish along with the bay leaves, cinnamon stick and garam masala: this will result in a wonderful deep, dark stock that the lamb chops will now cook in. Season very generously with salt. It is important that the mixture is quite salty at this stage, as it will lose its saltiness when the rice and chickpeas are added. Place a lid on the casserole dish and simmer the lamb chops in the stock for about 20 minutes.

Drain the soaked rice and rinse under cold running water, then add to the casserole with the chickpeas. Stir the rice into the stock by picking up the dish and swirling it around – try not use a spoon as this can release starch from the grains and make the final result 'gluey'.

A banquet given for Babur by the Mirzas, as depicted in the *Baburnama*.

Leave the rice to simmer, uncovered, in the stock over a medium heat for about 5 minutes while you preheat the oven to 200°C (180°C fan), gas mark 6. When the rice has absorbed most of the stock, place the lid back on the casserole dish and transfer to the oven for 8 minutes, then lower the heat to 120°C (100°C fan), gas mark ½. Cook for a further 8 minutes and then turn the oven off and leave the rice in the cooling oven for a further 25 minutes.

Serve the polow piping hot.

Qubooli Rice Salad

250g cooked rice (wild, brown or basmati)

250g cooked puy lentils

½ finely diced red onion, finely diced

½ cucumber, deseeded and diced

50g dried apricots, quartered

30g currants

50g pistachios, dry-roasted and roughly chopped

3 spring onions, thinly sliced

3 tablespoons extra virgin olive oil

Juice of 2 large lemons

1 red chilli, finely diced

2 tablespoons chopped fresh mint leaves

2 tablespoons chopped fresh coriander leaves

Sea salt, to taste

Emperor Aurangzeb often enjoyed a warm rice dish called *qubooli*, made from lentils, rice, dried fruit and nuts. Here, I have reinvented this dish in the form of a rice salad that is perfect for the summer months – light, flavoursome and punchy with sweet, spicy, nutty flavours.

———————————————

Put the rice and puy lentils into a bowl along with the red onion, cucumber, dried apricots, currants, pistachios and spring onions. Stir gently with a fork to combine.

Pour the olive oil, lemon juice, red chilli and a generous pinch of salt into a small jug and stir well with a fork. Drizzle this dressing over the rice and lentil salad, scatter over the mint and coriander and toss the salad gently to combine all the ingredients.

Serve at room temperature.

 NB *For an easy shortcut, use pouches of ready-cooked rice and lentils.*

Cashew Dum Biryani
with Potato & White Poppy Seeds

SERVES 6

400g basmati rice, soaked in water for at least 1 hour

3 green cardamom pods

6 cloves

1 small cinnamon stick

100ml light olive oil, plus extra for frying

2 onions, thinly sliced

8 garlic cloves, finely grated

50g grated ginger

½ teaspoon ground turmeric

1 teaspoon chilli flakes

½ teaspoon chilli powder

1 teaspoon garam masala

1 teaspoon ground coriander

1 teaspoon coarse black pepper

100g cashews

1 tablespoon white poppy seeds

400g Greek yoghurt

200ml warm water

2 tablespoons lemon juice

750g baby potatoes, halved or quartered if large

150g frozen peas, defrosted

Good pinch of saffron threads, steeped in 100ml warm milk

50g melted butter

2 tablespoons rose water

Salt, to taste

Although biryanis tend to be made with lamb, my version avoids meat, but still uses those same Mughal-inspired flavours. The fragrance in the kitchen as the biryani steams in the oven is enough to send any food enthusiast to gastronomic heaven. It is a fantastic accompaniment to any meat-based curry and is truly celebratory of the food of the Mughal era.

Drain the soaked rice and rinse thoroughly under the cold tap until the water runs clear. Bring a large pan of salted water to the boil. Add the rice, cardamom pods, cloves and cinnamon stick and cook for 5–7 minutes. The rice should be firm, but not entirely raw at this stage. Drain the parboiled rice and set aside, discarding the whole spices.

Heat the oil in a large pan, add the onions and cook over a medium heat for about 20 minutes, or until they are a dark golden brown colour. Add the garlic, ginger, turmeric, chilli flakes, chilli powder, garam masala, ground coriander and black pepper. Stir until the spices release their aromas, making sure the spices don't catch on the bottom of the pan.

Put the cashews and white poppy seeds into a food processor or blender and blitz to a powder; add this to onions and cook for 1–2 minutes. Add the Greek yoghurt and measured warm water to the pan and simmer gently for 5 minutes. Remove from the heat, add the lemon juice and plenty of salt and set aside to cool.

Heat a little oil in a frying pan and fry the baby potatoes over a medium heat until they are crisp and golden, about 5 minutes. Add to the onion/spice/cashew mixture with the peas.

Preheat the oven to 200°C (180°C fan), gas mark 6.

To assemble the biryani, start by layering the rice and potato mixture in a casserole dish. Ideally there should be at least five layers: rice, potato, rice,

NB *An alternative way to finish the biryani is to cover the final layer of rice with a sheet of puff pastry. Simply brush with beaten egg and bake in the oven as above.*

potato, rice. Combine the saffron-infused milk, melted butter and rose water in a jug and spoon this mixture evenly over the biryani.

Place the lid on top of the casserole dish and bake in the oven for about 30 minutes, or until the rice is cooked through and steam is rising from the biryani. Serve piping hot with your favourite meat-based curry.

Missi Pancakes

MAKES 6–8

180g gram flour

180g wholewheat flour

2 red onions, very thinly sliced

1 teaspoon ground coriander

½ tablespoon ajwain (carom) seeds

1 tablespoon dried fenugreek leaves

1 teaspoon chilli powder

4 tablespoons finely chopped fresh coriander

5 large eggs

300ml warm water

2 tablespoons olive oil

Ghee or butter, for frying

Salt, to taste

Missi roti is a spiced gram flour pancake that was a favourite of Emperor Bahadur Shah Zafar, and it's still extremely popular in south-east Asia today. They are traditionally made with just gram flour, spices and water and can have a very short texture, so in this recipe, I have added eggs to make a more pliable flatbread, almost like a pancake. The result is an earthy and wholesome bread with a very pleasing soft texture. I recommend eating them with a chutney, pickle or cool yoghurt.

Combine both flours, the onions, spices and fresh coriander in a large wide bowl. Season with a healthy pinch of salt. Put the eggs, measured warm water and olive oil into a jug and whisk until well combined. Pour this egg mixture into the bowl of flour and stir well to form a thick, sticky batter.

Place a non-stick pan over a medium heat. Drizzle a little ghee or butter into the pan and pour a couple of ladlefuls of the batter into the pan. Swirl the pan to ensure the batter spreads evenly – you are aiming for pancakes that are about 2–3mm thick. After 2–3 minutes flip the pancake over and brush the top with more ghee or butter. Cook for a couple of minutes until it is golden brown on both sides. Keep warm and repeat until all the batter is used, then serve immediately.

Radish & Mung Bean Parathas

MAKES 6

300g chapatti flour (or use half wholewheat flour and half plain flour), plus extra for dusting
1 teaspoon vegetable oil
1 teaspoon salt
Ghee or vegetable oil, for frying

For the Filling
200g pink radishes
150g cooked mung beans
1 medium cooked potato, peeled and chopped
1 green chilli (medium strength)
1 teaspoon cumin seeds
2 teaspoons anardana (pomegranate powder)
½ teaspoon chilli flakes
½ teaspoon chilli powder
1 teaspoon salt
2 tablespoons lemon juice
25g chopped fresh coriander

Parathas are fried wheat-flour flatbreads that can be stuffed with all manner of spicy fillings. They are traditionally made on a *tawa*, which is a flat skillet-like griddle. You can, of course, use a good-quality non-stick frying pan if you don't have a *tawa* at home. Parathas are best enjoyed piping hot with some cooling natural yoghurt.

Start by preparing the dough. Put all the ingredients, except the ghee or vegetable oil, into a large bowl and add just enough water to form a soft pliable dough. Knead by hand for 5 minutes, then divide the dough into six equal pieces, roll each one into a ball and return to the bowl. Cover the bowl with a cloth or cling film and set aside for 20 minutes.

Meanwhile, grate the radishes and squeeze them tightly between your hands to get rid of any excess moisture. Put into a bowl along with all the other filling ingredients and mix thoroughly so that the ingredients are well combined.

Take a piece of the dough, roll it into a perfect round between your hands and place it on a well-floured worktop. Use a rolling pin to roll the dough out to a circle about 15cm in diameter. Pile one-sixth of the filling into the centre of the dough circle and bring the sides of the dough up, pinching them at the top to seal in the filling. Turn the stuffed dough over so that the pinched side is face down. Gently roll the stuffed dough out again to a 15cm circle that is the thickness of a one pound coin. Don't worry if small bits of the stuffing start showing through – this is expected and adds to the final effect.

To cook the parathas, drizzle some ghee or vegetable oil into a skillet or non-stick frying pan set over a medium heat. Fry the parathas for 2–3 minutes each side. They should be golden and crisp. Serve immediately with a pickle or raita of your choice.

Afghani Potato & Spinach Bolani

300g plain flour, plus extra for dusting

1 tablespoon olive oil, plus extra for frying

1 teaspoon salt

100ml warm water

For the Filling

200g baby spinach leaves

250g mashed potato

50g spring onions, finely chopped

2 tablespoons finely chopped fresh coriander

2 tablespoons finely chopped fresh dill

1 teaspoon chilli flakes

Zest of 1 lemon

Salt, to taste

For the Dipping Sauce

300g Greek yoghurt

Juice of 1 lemon

4 fat garlic cloves, finely grated

2 tablespoons chopped fresh dill, plus a pinch to garnish

Drizzle of olive oil

Salt, to taste

Emperor Bahadur Shah Zafar was the last Mughal emperor. The culinary repertoire of his kitchen was particularly diverse, with Persian, Turkish and Afghan cuisine regularly finding their way onto the menu.

Bolani is typically eaten in Afghanistan, which was once ruled by the Mughal empire. These semicircular crispbreads with their vivid green spinach filling are just wonderful dipped into the punchy garlic and dill yoghurt sauce.

Start by preparing the dough. Put the flour, olive oil and salt into a bowl. Add the measured warm water to form a soft, pliable dough. Knead the dough by hand for 5 minutes, then divide into eight equal-sized dough balls, return to the bowl, cover with cling film and leave to rest for 20 minutes while you make the filling.

Wilt the spinach in a pan with just a splash of water. Allow it to cool and then squeeze out all the moisture and chop roughly. Add to a bowl with the mashed potato, spring onions, coriander, dill, chilli flakes and lemon zest. Mix well with a fork and add salt to taste.

To make the dipping sauce, pour the yoghurt into a bowl and season generously with salt. Stir in the lemon juice, garlic and dill. Drizzle some extra olive oil over the top and add a pinch of chopped dill.

To assemble the bolani, dust the worktop very lightly with flour. Roll each dough ball out with a rolling pin to a circle about 20cm in diameter (the dough will be quite thin, almost like a crêpe). Place the filling over one half of the dough and bring the other side over the filling to form a semicircle. Crimp the edges using a fork.

Drizzle olive oil into a non-stick frying pan or skillet and place over a medium heat. Fry the bolani for 2–3 minutes each side – they should be golden and crunchy all over. Serve with the yoghurt dipping sauce, either whole or cut into wedges (as pictured opposite).

Cheese, Cumin, Mint & Walnut Breads

with Saffron Butter

MAKES 6

425g strong white bread flour, plus extra for dusting

1 x 7g sachet of fast-action yeast

½ teaspoon salt

1 teaspoon sugar

250ml warm water

250g feta cheese, crumbled

1 heaped teaspoon cumin seeds, dry-roasted

1 teaspoon chilli flakes

4 tablespoons chopped fresh mint leaves, plus extra to garnish

1 tablespoon honey

50g walnuts, roughly chopped

1 teaspoon vegetable oil

Pinch of saffron threads, soaked in a few tablespoons of melted butter

Sea salt

Freshly cooked warm bread was a staple item of the Mughal kitchen. Ancient recipes from King Aurangzeb's era document breads that were stuffed with cottage cheese and curds. I use cumin, mint, walnuts and saffron to add a new flavour dimension.

Sift the flour into a bowl, add the yeast, salt and sugar and stir to combine. Add the measured warm water and knead by hand for about 5 minutes until it forms soft pliable dough. Cover the bowl with cling film and leave it to prove in a warm place for about 30 minutes until the dough has almost doubled in size. Meanwhile, put the feta, cumin seeds, chilli flakes, chopped mint, honey and walnuts into a bowl and stir to combine.

Dust a large piece of baking parchment liberally with flour. Divide the dough into six equal portions and then roll each one out on a lightly floured worktop to a diameter of 12–15cm. Carefully place one sixth of the cheese filling in the centre of the dough and gently bring the edges up and pinch together to form a ball. Turn the ball over onto the floured baking parchment so that the smooth surface faces upwards. Use a rolling pin to flatten the stuffed dough until it is about 1.5cm thick. Repeat with the remaining dough balls and filling.

Carefully transfer the breads, still on the baking parchment, to a baking tray. Rub the surface of the breads with the oil, sprinkle with some sea salt and a few mint leaves and allow to rest for 10 minutes while you preheat the oven to 200°C (180°C fan), gas mark 6.

Bake the breads for about 30 minutes, or until the breads are deep golden coloured. Brush with the saffron butter before serving.

NB *You can use paneer cheese, but I love salty cheese varieties like feta for that extra kick of flavour.*

Sour Cherry, Pistachio & Sesame Naan

MAKES 6

500g plain flour, plus extra for dusting

1 teaspoon baking powder

1 teaspoon bicarbonate of soda

1 tablespoon sugar

1 teaspoon salt

1 x 7g sachet of fast-action yeast

75g pistachios

75g dried sour cherries

200ml warm milk

150g natural yoghurt

Ghee or melted butter, for greasing and brushing

6 teaspoons black sesame seeds

The sweet nutty tones of this naan bread are particularly well suited to the spicy sweet flavours of meat and poultry dishes cooked by the Mughals. You can substitute for other dried fruits and nuts, for example, apricots, sultanas, almonds, cashews, walnuts or prunes.

Put the flour, baking powder, bicarbonate of soda, sugar, salt and yeast into a large bowl and add the pistachios and sour cherries. Stir these dry ingredients well with a fork.

Heat the milk in a pan until it is warm, but not hot enough to scald. Add the yoghurt and milk to the dry ingredients and combine well to form a soft pliable dough. Knead the dough by hand for 5 minutes on a well-floured surface. Return the dough to the bowl, cover with cling film and put in a warm place for 45 minutes, or until the dough has roughly doubled in size.

Grease three baking trays with ghee or melted butter. Divide the dough into six equal-sized balls. Dust the worktop with flour and roll each dough ball into a circle about 15cm in diameter and 1cm thick. Place the breads on the baking trays – you should get two breads on each one. Finally brush some more ghee over the surface of the breads and sprinkle over the sesame seeds. Cover with cling film and allow to rest for 10 minutes while you preheat the oven to 220°C (200°C fan), gas mark 7.

Bake the breads for 8–12 minutes until they have puffed up and are a beautiful rich golden colour. Remove from the oven and serve immediately. If you want to eat these later, wrap them in a tea towel – they will stay soft for a couple of hours.

Pickles, Relishes & Raitas

Great precautions were taken to ensure the purity of dishes being served to the Mughal emperors. After all, transporting food from the kitchens to the dining area was nothing short of a Herculean task. Gold and silver dishes sent from the imperial kitchen were sealed with special red cloth, while white cloth was used for copper and china dishes. The servants in the pantry would also send large bags up to the dining area containing a variety of curds, raitas, pickles, fresh ginger and green chillies. These would accompany the banquet so each diner could pick and choose their favourite condiments.

Emperor Bahadur Shah Zafar was particularly fond of spiced mango pickle. His friend, prime minister and personal physician Hakim Ahsanullah Khan banned him from eating this pickle because it caused him digestive discomfort. When Emperor Zafar ignored his advice, Hakim was very annoyed, saying, 'if the King would act this way he had better dismiss me at once'. Emperor Zafar was forced to apologise and promise greater abstinence in the future. Amusing to think a pickle could have caused such a ruckus…

The pickles, relishes and raitas in this chapter can accompany almost any of the meat, vegetable and rice dishes in this book, although they are also particularly wonderful as part of a spread, to dip into with flatbreads or poppadums.

Kashmiri Plum & Almond Chutney

SERVES 10–12

450g dried Kashmiri plums
200g caster sugar
1 teaspoon ground ginger
2 green cardamom pods, bruised
1 tablespoon char maghaz (raw white melon seeds)
1 red chilli, finely diced
50g blanched almonds
350ml warm water
Salt, to taste

This sweet and sour chutney always finds its way onto the table at traditional Pakistani wedding feasts. It is enjoyed alongside biryani, kebabs and fresh bread from the tandoor oven. Dried Kashmiri plums are wonderfully tart with a flavour not dissimilar to tamarind – they can be found online or in your local Asian supermarket.

———————————

First sterilise a jar: wash the jar and its lid thoroughly in warm soapy water and then placing in an oven preheated to 140°C (120°C fan), gas mark 1 for 5 minutes, or until no moisture remains.

Put all the ingredients into a pan and simmer over a low heat for 45 minutes, stirring occasionally. The chutney is ready when it has a sticky, syrupy consistency and the Kashmiri plums have rehydrated. Take care not to reduce the chutney too much as it will thicken as it cools.

Allow to cool slightly before transferring to your sterilised jar. The chutney will keep for a couple of months; store in the fridge once opened.

Blackberry & Star Anise Chutney

SERVES 6

150g muscovado sugar

½ red onion, chopped

4–6 star anise

1 cinnamon stick

300g blackberries

100g dried sour cherries

1 tablespoon grated ginger

1 teaspoon chilli flakes

1 teaspoon cumin seeds, dry-roasted

100ml orange juice

200ml apple vinegar

Salt, to taste

There is something wonderfully festive about this chutney. It would make an excellent accompaniment to roast turkey at Thanksgiving or Christmas. This will keep for about a month in the fridge in a sterilised jar.

First sterilise a jar: wash the jar and its lid thoroughly in warm soapy water and then placing in an oven preheated to 140°C (120°C fan), gas mark 1 for 5 minutes, or until no moisture remains.

Put two-thirds of the blackberries into a pan with all the remaining ingredients. Simmer over a low heat for 30–45 minutes, or until the sauce has thickened and the fruit has broken down completely. Add the remaining blackberries to the chutney a few minutes before removing from the heat (this will give the final dish the contrasting texture of smooth and whole blackberries). The chutney will thicken as it cools, so do not reduce it down too much.

You can pick out the star anise and cinnamon before transferring to your sterilised jar, but I like to leave them in for authenticity and added flavour.

Both recipes are illustrated overleaf.

Mango, Strawberry & Tamarind Chutney

SERVES 6

1 heaped teaspoon brown sugar

3 tablespoons tamarind pulp

1 teaspoon cumin seeds,
dry-roasted and ground

½ teaspoon black pepper

75ml water

150g peeled and diced fresh
mango

200g strawberries, diced

A fabulous south-east-Asian-style sweet and sour sauce. This is perfect in the summer when strawberries and mangoes are both at their best and makes a great little accompaniment to poppadums at the beginning of your meal.

————————

Put the sugar, tamarind, cumin seeds and black pepper into a pan, add the measured water and mix well. Simmer over a low heat until the mixture has thickened and has a saucy consistency, then set aside to cool.

Add the diced mango and strawberries and stir well to combine. This is a fresh chutney so is best enjoyed within a few hours.

KASHMIRI PLUM
& ALMOND
CHUTNEY

BLACKBERRY &
STAR ANISE
CHUTNEY

MANGO, STRAWBERRY
& TAMARIND CHUTNEY

Whipped Walnut Relish

SERVES 4–6

350g full-fat Greek yoghurt

100g walnuts, soaked in water for 1 hour, plus a few crushed walnuts to garnish

½ onion, roughly chopped

1 green chilli

½ teaspoon cumin seeds

Drizzle of extra virgin olive oil

Salt, to taste

The walnut, with all its full-bodied, bittersweet oily magnificence, was imported from afar and enjoyed extensively in the Mughal era – there are historical records of walnuts being piled high in Mughal markets. Emperor Babur spent much time in Kabul and it was here that he is said to have enjoyed walnuts in the winter months. This walnut relish is particularly wonderful served with game, duck and roast beef.

_____

First tip the yoghurt into the centre of a muslin cloth or clean J-cloth and suspend it over a bowl in the fridge for 2–3 hours, to drain away the excess liquid.

Drain the walnuts and add to a food processor or blender with the onion, green chilli and cumin seeds and blend with a few tablespoons of the yoghurt until it is completely smooth. Add the remaining yogurt and season with salt. Transfer to a bowl and garnish with a few crushed walnuts and a generous drizzle of extra virgin olive oil.

Mint & Pomegranate Dip

SERVES 6

75g dried pomegranate seeds
(available online or from Asian
supermarkets)
25g fresh mint leaves
30g fresh coriander leaves
1 green chilli
1 teaspoon sugar
Juice of 1 large lemon
Salt, to taste

A classic Pakistani dip that is great with pakoras, samosas, any barbecued red meat or skewered kebabs. Traditionally it was painstakingly prepared in a pestle and mortar, but a food processor provides a very easy shortcut.

———————————————

Put all the ingredients into a mini food processor or blender. Add a few splashes of water and blitz to form a smooth sauce.

When it is ready to serve, the deep emerald green chutney will have a very slightly grainy texture from the pomegranate seeds. Keep in the fridge in an airtight container for up to 3 days.

Rose, Sultana & Ginger Relish

SERVES 6

100g golden sultanas

100g dried apricots

1 teaspoon grated ginger

1 teaspoon cumin seeds, dry-roasted

2 tablespoons rose water

3 drops of rose extract

Juice of 1 lemon

1 green chilli

1 teaspoon caster sugar

Salt, to taste

This relish is a beautiful accompaniment to chicken or any other white meat. The unusual combination of hot and sweet works surprisingly well, and the addition of rose water brings a delicate floral undertone to the palate.

First sterilise a jar: wash the jar and its lid thoroughly in warm soapy water and then placing in an oven preheated to 140°C (120°C fan), gas mark 1 for 5 minutes, or until no moisture remains.

Soak the sultanas and apricots in hot water for 15 minutes.

Drain the sultanas and apricots and add to a food processor or blender with all the remaining ingredients and just enough water to form a smooth purée.

Transfer the purée to a pan and simmer gently for 5 minutes – this helps amalgamate the flavours and gives a smooth, glossy finish. Transfer to your sterilised jar, seal with the lid and keep in the fridge for up to 2 weeks.

Both recipes are illustrated overleaf.

MINT &
POMEGRANATE
DIP

ROSE, SULTANA
& GINGER RELISH

CORIANDER,
CASHEW
& GOLDEN
SULTANA DIP

Coriander, Cashew & Golden Sultana Dip

SERVES 6

125g raw cashews
125g golden sultanas
60g chopped coriander
1 green bullet chilli (see Note)
75ml lemon juice
Salt, to taste

This is the recipe for my famous green chutney! Extremely versatile and a complete explosion of flavour. I have been known to eat spoonfuls of this at night when the craving arises. I use one chilli for an undertone of heat, but if you like your chutney very hot, feel free to add more.

─────────────

First sterilise a jar: wash the jar and its lid thoroughly in warm soapy water and then placing in an oven preheated to 140°C (120°C fan), gas mark 1 for 5 minutes, or until no moisture remains.

Soak the cashews and sultanas in cold water for 30 minutes.

Drain the sultanas and cashews and put them into a mini food processor or blender with the remaining ingredients. Add a few splashes of water and blitz to as smooth a consistency as you can. Season to taste with salt and transfer to your sterilised jar.

This chutney will keep for 3–5 days in the fridge but should be served at room temperature, so remove from the fridge an hour before serving.

 NB *Bullet chillies are very hot Indian chillies; if you can't find them use 2 green finger chillies instead.*

Eastern Cauliflower Piccalilli

SERVES 8

300g cauliflower florets
1 lemon, thinly sliced
3 large green chillies, sliced lengthways
150g sugar
150ml cider vinegar
100ml water
½ teaspoon ground turmeric
½ teaspoon asafoetida
1 teaspoon mustard seeds
1 teaspoon chilli flakes
1 teaspoon coriander seeds
50g fresh ginger, peeled and cut into julienne
1 heaped teaspoon sea salt
100ml olive oil

A wonderful sweet and sour pickle that I love eating with chapattis and parathas. It provides an instant hit of flavour and texture, which always pleases. It is best enjoyed after a week – if you can wait that long!

———————————

First sterilise a large jar: wash the jar and its lid thoroughly in warm soapy water and then placing in an oven preheated to 140°C (120°C fan), gas mark 1 for 5 minutes, or until no moisture remains.

Slice each cauliflower floret into slices about 1cm thick and add to your sterilised jar along with the lemon slices and green chillies.

To make the pickling liquid, put the sugar, vinegar, measured water, turmeric, asafoetida, mustard seeds, chilli flakes, coriander seeds, ginger and salt into a pan. Bring to the boil and then boil vigorously until it has reduced by approximately half. Pour the pickling liquid over the cauliflowers in the jar, followed by the olive oil. Seal the jar tightly, then shake it around gently to ensure that all the cauliflower pieces are coated with the pickling liquid.

Leave the pickle in a cool place for at least 24 hours before enjoying it, although it is even better after a week. The cauliflowers will release moisture as they pickle so don't worry if it seems like there is not enough pickling liquid in the jar to start with. Once opened store in the fridge and keep for up to a month.

 NB *This recipe is the perfect accompaniment to my Nargisi Kofta Scotch Eggs, as pictured on page 50.*

Pumpkin, Honey & Saffron Raita

SERVES 6–8

400g pumpkin, peeled, deseeded and cut into cubes

10 garlic cloves, peeled but left whole

500g full-fat Greek yoghurt

2 tablespoons honey

2 tablespoons golden sultanas

½ teaspoon saffron threads, soaked in a few tablespoons of warm water

½ teaspoon chilli flakes

Salt, to taste

Pumpkin is such a lovely autumnal vegetable and comes in a variety of colours and shapes. The combination of honey, garlic and saffron is traditionally Kashmiri, a region once part of the Mughal empire. This dip works particularly well with Turmeric Roast Potatoes (see page 81) or roast butternut squash, or even just warm flatbreads.

———————————

Bring a large pan of water to the boil and add the pumpkin cubes and garlic cloves. Cook until the pumpkin can be pierced easily with a knife, about 25 minutes. Drain in a colander and set aside to cool.

Meanwhile, put the yoghurt, honey, sultanas, saffron and its soaking water and chilli flakes into a food processor or blender.

When the pumpkin and garlic are completely cool, add to the food processor or blender and blitz thoroughly to form a smooth, full-bodied purée. Season to taste with salt.

Turmeric Aubergine
& Tadka Yoghurt Raita

SERVES 4

1 large aubergine, cut into 5mm slices

75ml olive oil, plus extra for brushing

½ teaspoon ground turmeric

200g natural yoghurt, at room temperature

1 tablespoon honey

2 garlic cloves, thinly sliced

1 teaspoon cumin seeds

1 red chilli, finely diced

2 tablespoons finely chopped fresh coriander

2 tablespoons thinly sliced fresh mint leaves

Handful of pomegranate seeds

Salt, to taste

This gently spiced aubergine raita dish is wonderful served alongside warm flatbreads. You can use the bread to scoop up the soft aubergines and sweet, spiced yoghurt.

———————————

Liberally brush each aubergine slice with olive oil until they are coated all over. Now sprinkle turmeric and a good pinch of salt over the aubergines so that all the aubergines have taken on the vibrant yellow of the turmeric.

Place a large non-stick pan over a medium-high heat and fry the aubergine slices in batches for about 4–5 minutes on each side. They should be completely soft and caramelised on both sides. Arrange the aubergines in a single layer on a large flat platter.

Put the yoghurt and honey into a bowl and whisk with a fork until smooth. Season to taste with salt.

Pour the 75ml olive oil into a frying pan and place over a high heat; when it is very hot, but not quite smoking, add the garlic, cumin seeds and diced chilli – the garlic and cumin should start colouring very quickly. When they are golden brown, remove from the heat and pour carefully over the yoghurt; stir well.

Drizzle the yoghurt mix over the aubergines and scatter over the coriander, mint and pomegranate seeds.

Smoky Eastern Ketchup

SERVES 6

400g cherry tomatoes, halved

3 garlic cloves, peeled but left whole

1 green chilli

Olive oil, for brushing

50g soft brown sugar

4 tablespoons cider vinegar

This ketchup is fabulous with chips, pakoras, samosas or any other deep-fried delights.

————————————

Preheat the grill to high.

Place the halved tomatoes skin-side up on a baking tray along with the garlic cloves and chilli. Brush the tomatoes, garlic and chilli with olive oil and grill for 3–5 minutes until the tomatoes are very dark and charred.

Transfer the charred tomatoes, garlic and chilli to a food processor or blender and blitz to form a smoky purée. Transfer to a small pan, add the remaining ingredients and simmer over a low heat for 15 minutes until the sauce is thick and sticky with the texture of ketchup.

Sweets

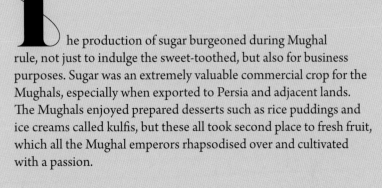

The production of sugar burgeoned during Mughal rule, not just to indulge the sweet-toothed, but also for business purposes. Sugar was an extremely valuable commercial crop for the Mughals, especially when exported to Persia and adjacent lands. The Mughals enjoyed prepared desserts such as rice puddings and ice creams called kulfis, but these all took second place to fresh fruit, which all the Mughal emperors rhapsodised over and cultivated with a passion.

When Emperor Babur moved from central Asia to India, he was particularly unimpressed by the small melons and immediately set about importing large melons from further afield. Premium-quality fruit was wrapped in cotton wool and carried from Samarkand, Afghanistan and Kashmir into Delhi by a series of coordinated runners. The famous Chandni Chowk marketplace in Delhi was home to the 'fruit wallahs', who sold an array of fruit grown on the fertile lands of the empire.

The simple act of giving and receiving sweetmeats was an important social convention in Mughal India. Sweetmeats, also known as halwas, were made from premium-quality cashews, pistachios, carrots, almonds, pulses, coconut and copious amounts of sugar. These halwas are just as popular in south-east Asia today.

I was lucky enough to visit the sweetmeat shops of Chandni Chowk on my last trip to Delhi. The confectioners told me the most fascinating tale: legend dictates that one of Delhi's last Mughal emperors was so fond of the sweetmeats of Chandni Chowk that he would personally visit the shops atop his imperial elephant. One summer day the royal elephant craved sweetmeats and so made its own way to Chandni Chowk, not returning to the palace until it was given its fill of sweets by the shopkeeper. Of course, I cannot say whether there is any truth in this tale, but it certainly is a novel story.

I have included a variety of desserts in this chapter, varying from the luxuriously rich to the light and fruity. The flavours of cardamom, rose water and floral scents predominate and serve as a wonderful end to any Mughal feast.

Infused with Hibiscus, Fennel & Cardamom

Watermelon

SERVES 4–6

20g dried hibiscus leaves (look online or in Middle Eastern supermarkets)

10g fennel seeds

100g caster sugar

5 cardamom pods, bruised

500ml water

750g chilled watermelon, cut into large chunks

The emperors are known to have become quite misty-eyed in their love for fruit and numerous historical accounts narrate the Mughal fondness for watermelon. The sweet fruitiness of hibiscus and aniseed tones of fennel and cardamom make the most wonderful vivid pink syrup, which the watermelon soaks up like a sponge.

———————————

Put the hibiscus leaves, fennel seeds, sugar, cardamom pods and measured water into a pan and place over a medium heat. Cook for 20–30 minutes, or until the mixture has reduced down to a maple-syrup-like consistency. Note that the syrup will thicken as it cools so take care not to reduce too much, although you can always loosen it with a few tablespoons of water. Set aside to cool.

Arrange the watermelon on a large platter. Strain the cooled hibiscus syrup over the watermelon and allow it to steep for about 20 minutes before serving.

Saffron-poached Apple Murabba

SERVES 4–6

1 litre apple juice (clear not cloudy)

220ml caster sugar

Pared rind of 1 orange

1 cinnamon stick

Good pinch of saffron threads

10 cardamom pods, bruised

4 large or 6 small Braeburn apples, peeled

2 tablespoons rose water

Lightly whipped double cream, yoghurt or ice cream, to serve

To Decorate (optional)

4 or 6 sheets of edible silver leaf

Handful of toasted flaked almonds

This recipe is in honour of my grandmother, who loved to eat and cook with apples. In Pakistan, you can buy tins of candied apples called *murabba*; there are varieties made with and without saffron. Interestingly, the tradition of preserving fruits in sugar is indeed a Mughal one. These apples are very sweet and rich, a perfect accompaniment to yoghurt, ice cream or lightly whipped double cream.

Combine the apple juice, sugar, orange rind, cinnamon stick, saffron threads and cardamom pods in a large, heavy-based pan set over a medium heat. Bring the mixture to the boil, stirring until sugar is dissolved.

Add the apples to the syrup and simmer over a medium heat for 25–30 minutes until they are tender when pierced with a sharp knife. Rotate the apples occasionally to ensure that they cook evenly.

Using a slotted spoon, transfer the apples to a serving dish. Continue to simmer the syrup left in the pan until about a cup of syrup remains in the pan. Add the rose water to the pan, then strain the syrup into a jug – it should have the consistency of maple syrup. If you find that the syrup is too thick (as it often becomes thicker as it cools), loosen the mixture down with a few tablespoons of water.

Spoon the saffron syrup over the apples. Decorate each poached apple with edible silver leaf and toasted almonds, if liked. Serve with lightly whipped double cream, yoghurt or ice cream.

Crème Fraîche & Rose Ice Cream
with Honey-glazed Figs

225ml whole milk

150g caster sugar

6 large egg yolks

450g crème fraîche

3–5 tablespoons rose water (depending on how strong you like it), plus extra to serve

50ml lemon juice

8 fresh ripe figs, halved lengthways

4 tablespoons honey

Handful of dried rose petals, to decorate

Historical accounts describe how the desserts of this era relied heavily on the inventive use of dairy products. Milk was often slowly heated to a sticky, condensed milk consistency, at which point fruits and nuts were added. This recipe pays tribute to the dairy-based dessert tradition of the Mughals. I use crème fraîche scented with rose water as a much lighter and healthier alternative to condensed milk, but a good-quality Greek yoghurt would do just as well.

Warm honey-glazed figs perfumed with rose water are a wonderful way of counterbalancing the slightly sharp, chilled crème fraîche, making this the perfect palate-cleansing end to a rich Mughal meal.

Put the milk and sugar into a pan, place over a low heat and cook, stirring, until the sugar dissolves.

Whisk the egg yolks in a bowl and slowly pour over the hot milk, stirring continuously to avoid curdling. Transfer this mixture to a clean pan and simmer, stirring continuously, over a very low heat for about 8–10 minutes until the mixture has thickened to a custard consistency. Immediately transfer the custard to a clean bowl and put into the fridge to cool.

Add the crème fraîche to the cooled custard along with the rose water and lemon juice. Pass the mixture through a sieve to remove any lumps and then transfer to an ice cream machine. Churn according to the manufacturer's instructions. Transfer to a plastic container and freeze for at least 1 hour before serving. (Alternatively, if you don't have an ice cream machine, pour the mixture into a plastic container and put into the freezer. After 30 minutes transfer to a food processor or blender and blitz to break up the ice crystals, then return to the freezer. Repeat this process three or four more times.)

Meanwhile, preheat the oven to 200°C (180°C fan), gas mark 6. Put the halved figs into a small roasting tin, drizzle over the honey and bake for 10–12 minutes until the figs have softened. Remove from the oven and sprinkle over a few drops of rose water.

Serve the crème fraîche ice cream with the warm rose-scented figs and decorated with the dried rose petals.

Sandalwood Ice Cream

SERVES 4–6

300ml whole milk
300ml double cream
200ml sandal syrup
1 teaspoon ground cardamom
6 egg yolks
Handful of pistachios,
toasted and chopped, to decorate

Sandal syrup is the concentrated herbal syrup made from the extract of sandalwood. If you recognise the fragrance of sandalwood you can almost guess how it will taste. You can buy it ready-made in bottles from Asian food shops.

As children, we were given ice-cold glasses of sandal sherbet drink on blisteringly hot summer days in order to quench our thirst. The woody, exotic, floral taste is quite spectacular and takes extremely well to being made into ice cream.

Pour the milk and double cream into a pan and bring it to the boil. Remove the pan from the heat and allow the contents to cool a little. Add the sandal syrup and ground cardamom to the hot cream and milk mixture and stir well.

Put the egg yolks into a large clean bowl and whisk well until light and fluffy. Pour the hot milk onto the egg yolks and whisk constantly so that the egg yolks and milk are well combined. If the milk is too hot at this stage the egg will curdle so be careful to not overheat it.

Transfer the mixture to a clean pan and reheat gently, stirring continuously with a wooden spoon. The custard is ready when it coats the back of a spoon, or if you have a thermometer, when it reaches 80°C. Take care not to overheat, as again the mixture will curdle.

Finally, for the smoothest possible finish, pass the custard through a sieve and allow it to cool before transferring to an ice cream machine to churn according to the manufacturer's instructions. (Alternatively, you can transfer to your freezer and whisk vigorously every 30 minutes for 3 hours to prevent any crystals from forming.)

Serve scoops of the sandalwood ice cream decorated with chopped toasted pistachios.

Shahi Tukre

SERVES 4

About 75g ghee or butter

8 slices of white bread

500ml milk

Pinch of saffron threads

1 cinnamon stick

8 cloves

8 black peppercorns

2 star anise

2 eggs

120g caster sugar

1 tablespoon pistachios, dry-roasted and chopped

1 tablespoon flaked almonds, dry-roasted and chopped

4 chopped dried apricots

Shahi tukre is the Mughal version of bread and butter pudding. The term *shahi* translates as 'royal' in Urdu and *tukre* means 'piece or bite'. The Mughals would break their fast with this dessert in the month of Ramadan, and this tradition persists in parts of south-east Asia today.

Interestingly, in the original Mughal version of the dish, the imperial cooks did not use eggs – the bread was fried and then doused in sugar syrup and topped with thickened milk. I've used eggs here as I feel it enhances the final texture of this regal dish.

_____

Spread the ghee or butter on both sides of the bread slices. Place the buttered bread in a non-stick pan and fry over a medium heat until they are golden brown on both sides. Cut each slice of bread into four triangles and arrange them neatly in an ovenproof dish.

Pour the milk into a pan together with the saffron, cinnamon, cloves, peppercorns and star anise. Allow the milk to infuse with the spices over a low heat for about 25 minutes. Strain the milk to remove the spices and allow it to cool slightly.

Put the eggs and sugar into a bowl and whisk them gently together. Slowly pour the warm milk over the eggs and sugar and whisk to combine (make sure the milk is not too hot as the mixture will curdle otherwise). Pour the custard mixture over the fried bread, ensuring each piece of bread is coated. Set aside to rest while you preheat the oven to 200°C (180°C fan), gas mark 6.

Bake for about 25 minutes, or until it looks crisp and deep golden. Scatter the pistachios, almonds and apricots over the finished pudding and serve hot or warm, with double cream.

Buttermilk, Saffron & Orange Blossom Panna Cotta

with Candied Pistachios

SERVES 4

250ml double cream

120g caster sugar

½ teaspoon saffron threads, soaked in a few tablespoons of warm water

3 tablespoons orange blossom water

½ teaspoon ground cardamom

2½ sheets of platinum-strength leaf gelatine

250ml buttermilk

For the Candied Pistachios

100g granulated sugar

100g shelled pistachios

Vegetable oil, for greasing

NB *You can of course replace the orange blossom water with rose water, or use a combination of floral scents if you prefer.*

You will not be able to resist this one. The slight lactic acidity of buttermilk is particularly special with the earthy notes of saffron and heady perfume of orange blossom water.

Heat the double cream and sugar in a pan until it just comes to boiling point. Take the cream off the heat and add the saffron and its soaking water, orange blossom water and ground cardamom. Allow the cream to cool slightly.

Soften the gelatine by soaking it in some warm water. When the gelatine is very soft, squeeze out the moisture and drop it into the warm cream mixture. The gelatine should dissolve immediately into the cream. Working quickly, combine the buttermilk with the cream mixture. Give the mixture a final taste; you can add more orange blossom water, saffron or cardamom at this point, if you like. Pour the panna cotta mixture into four individual ramekins. Transfer to the fridge to set for at least 4 hours, ideally overnight.

Meanwhile, make the candied pistachios. Melt the sugar in a pan over a medium heat until it turns to a deep-brown-coloured caramel, swirling the pan occasionally to melt it evenly. Quickly add the pistachios to the caramel, stir once to ensure the pistachios are all coated and pour the whole mixture onto a piece of greased baking parchment and set aside to cool.

Roughly chop the caramelised pistachios and sprinkle over the smooth, wobbly panna cotta as a crunchy accompaniment.

with Dark Chocolate & Rose Cream
Turkish Delight Pots

SERVES 6

150g butter, plus extra for greasing
160g dark chocolate
4 eggs
200g soft light brown sugar
75g plain flour, plus extra for dusting
About 150g Turkish delight, chopped into small chunks

For the Rose Cream
150ml double cream
2 tablespoons Turkish rose petal jam

No cookery book is complete without a really brilliant chocolate dessert recipe. While I am aware that chocolate was not on Mughal menus, rose water most definitely was. The surprise ingredient in these chocolate pots is the rose-flavoured Turkish delight – it is quite spectacular as it melts in the oven to become a molten rosy syrup.

Preheat the oven to 200°C (180°C fan), gas mark 6.

Put the butter and chocolate into a heatproof bowl and set over a pan of gently simmering water. Stir the butter and chocolate together with a spatula until melted and set aside.

Whisk the eggs, sugar and flour together gently in a large bowl. Now pour the melted chocolate and butter mixture into the bowl and stir well to combine.

Grease and flour six ramekins. Place a few pieces of chopped-up Turkish delight into each ramekin and top with the chocolate mixture. Place the ramekins on a baking tray and bake in the oven for 10–12 minutes.

Meanwhile, make the rose cream. Whisk the double cream till it forms soft peaks. Drizzle over the rose petal jam and gently swirl into the cream to create a rippled effect. Serve with the chocolate pots.

Emperor's Mango Shrikhand Pudding

1kg full-fat Greek yoghurt

50g icing sugar

1 teaspoon saffron threads, soaked in a few tablespoons of warm water

Handful of whole almonds, dry-roasted and chopped

Handful of pistachios, dry-roasted and chopped

1 large mango, peeled, stoned and cut into 1.5cm-thick slices

2 tablespoons caster sugar

½ teaspoon chilli flakes

Small knob of butter

The famous Persian poet Amir Khusrau called mango the fairest fruit of Hindustan. The Mughals were fervent mango lovers and their memoirs talk of their love for mangoes extensively. They cultivated varieties of mangoes such as the famous Totapuri mango, which was allegedly the first to be exported to Persia and adjacent kingdoms.

Emperor Shah Jahan and Emperor Jahangir were also known to financially reward those cooks who came up with the best mango dishes. Shrikhand is a yoghurt-based dessert; the addition of mango, a hint of chilli and saffron is spectacular.

Put the yoghurt in the centre of a muslin cloth or clean J-cloth and hang overnight in the fridge to drain away some of the liquid. Make sure you place a bowl underneath to catch the liquid.

Tip the hung yoghurt into a bowl and add the icing sugar and saffron and its soaking water. Stir well to combine using a spatula. Pour the yoghurt into a shallow serving dish.

Sprinkle the sliced mango with the caster sugar and chilli flakes. Melt the butter in a non-stick frying pan over a medium heat, add the mango slices and cook until they are caramelised and golden brown on the outside, but still holding their shape.

Carefully place the slices of caramelised mango over the platter of yoghurt and scatter over the nuts. Serve immediately.

with Honeycomb & Clotted Cream

Dates

SERVES 4

140g clotted cream

½ teaspoon ground cardamom

500g soft dates, e.g. Medjool

Handful of whole almonds (1–2 almonds per date), dry-roasted

1 tablespoon pistachios, dry-roasted and chopped, to decorate

For the Honeycomb

100g caster sugar

100g liquid glucose (look in the baking aisle of the supermarket)

30g golden syrup

8g bicarbonate of soda

This is a fantastic little treat to go with a cup of coffee. The honeycomb and almonds give these bite-sized delights the most wonderful crunch.

_____

First make the honeycomb. Put the caster sugar, liquid glucose and golden syrup into a pan and place over a medium heat until a deep golden brown caramel forms, swirling the pan occasionally so that the mixture colours evenly. Take the pan off the heat and scatter over the bicarbonate of soda. The mixture will froth up immediately. Pour the frothing mixture quickly onto a piece of baking parchment or a silicone sheet. Allow the mixture to cool and once it is completely hard, break it into pieces.

Put the clotted cream into a bowl with the cardamom and stir well to combine. Remove the stone from each date and stuff each one with clotted cream. Gently push an almond into the cream centre of the dates. Decorate the dates with chunks of honeycomb and some chopped pistachios for colour. (Don't add the honeycomb until just before serving, so that it stays crisp.)

Carrot Halwa Cake

200g light brown muscovado sugar

3 eggs

250ml sunflower oil

50ml milk

300g plain flour

1 teaspoon baking powder

1 teaspoon bicarbonate of soda

50g butter, plus extra for greasing

100g caster sugar

400g grated carrots

1 teaspoon ground cinnamon

½ teaspoon ground cardamom

1 teaspoon ground ginger

75g pistachios, roughly chopped

25g whole almonds, roughly chopped

25g cashews, roughly chopped

25g golden sultanas

For the Icing

300g cream cheese, at room temperature

125g icing sugar

140ml double cream

Carrot halwa was a delicacy in the Mughal era and is still a classic celebratory dessert in south-east Asia. Carrots are slowly cooked in butter, sugar and nuts to create the most wonderful candied carrot mixture. This carrot cake has been made in honour of the carrot halwa – the flavours are very much reminiscent of the classic Mughal dessert.

Preheat the oven to 190°C (170°C fan), gas mark 5 and grease two 20cm cake tins.

Mix the muscovado sugar, eggs, sunflower oil and milk in a large bowl and whisk until well combined. Sift the flour, baking powder and bicarbonate of soda into a separate bowl and set aside.

To make the carrot halwa, melt the butter and caster sugar in a pan until the sugar has dissolved. When the butter is foaming, add the grated carrots, stir well and cook for about 5 minutes. Add the ground spices to the just softened carrots. Finally, add 25g of the pistachios, the almonds, cashews and sultanas to the carrots, stir to combine and then set aside to cool.

To finish the cake batter, tip the sifted dry ingredients and the carrot halwa into the bowl of wet ingredients and stir thoroughly with a wooden spoon. Pour the cake batter evenly into the prepared cake tins and bake in the oven for 30–40 minutes. The cake will be ready when a knife inserted into the centre of the cake comes out clean (or with just a few crumbs sticking to it). Remove the cakes from the oven and allow them to cool completely.

To make the icing, put the cream cheese in a bowl and beat using a hand-held electric whisk for about 15 seconds, or until the cheese is smooth. Add the icing sugar and cream and beat again until it is incorporated, and appears thick and smooth.

Illustrated overleaf (from left to right):

Dates with Honeycomb & Clotted Cream; Almond Khatai Biscuits; Masala Chai; Carrot Halwa Cake; Cumin, Turmeric & Ajwain Nimki Straws; and Mughal Spiced Nut Mix.

To assemble the cake, turn the cooled cakes over so that the flat surface is uppermost (this makes spreading the icing easier). However, if you find that your cakes have 'domed' in the centre, use a long bread knife to slice off the top to make them more even. Use a palette knife to spread about a third of the icing over the surface of one cake and sandwich together with the other cake. Spread the remaining icing over the top of the cake and down the sides as well. Finish by pressing the remaining pistachios onto the icing on top of the cake.

Almond Khatai Biscuits

MAKES 15–18

100g whole almonds

200g plain flour, plus extra for dusting

1½ tablespoons gram flour

½ teaspoon ground cardamom

2 teaspoons baking powder

½ teaspoon bicarbonate of soda

Pinch of salt

110g ghee or butter

100g icing sugar

2 egg yolks

Khatai biscuits were a popular biscuit in my grandmother's home. They would arrive in cardboard boxes from the local bakery and were eaten with hot cups of sweet tea in the morning. They were dangerously crumbly, sweet and full of crunchy toasted almonds. I can best describe them as a sort of eastern almond shortbread.

———————————

Preheat the oven to 200°C (180°C fan), gas mark 6. Put the almonds on a roasting tray and toast them in the oven for about 10–12 minutes, or until they are a deep golden brown colour. Allow the almonds to cool and then chop them up into small pieces.

Combine the plain flour, gram flour, cardamom, baking powder, bicarbonate of soda and salt in a large bowl and set aside.

Put the ghee or butter into a large bowl and then place in the freezer for 15 minutes so that it hardens slightly. Using a hand-held electric whisk, cream the icing sugar into the ghee or butter until the mixture is pale yellow.

Now add the chopped toasted almonds and dry ingredients to the creamed ghee/butter and sugar mixture together with 1 egg yolk. Add just enough ice-cold water (about a tablespoon) to bring the mixture together into a short, crumbly dough.

Dust your worktop with a little flour and roll out the mixture with a rolling pin until it is about 1cm thick. Use a round 5cm cutter to make about 15–18 biscuits. Use a palette knife to carefully transfer the biscuits to a baking tray lined with baking parchment. Chill in the fridge for at least 30 minutes.

When you are ready to bake, preheat the oven to 170°C (150°C fan), gas mark 3. Beat the remaining egg yolk in a bowl, then use a pastry brush to brush the egg yolk over the centre of the biscuits. Bake for about 25–30 minutes, or until a light golden brown colour. Cool on the baking tray (they are delicate so don't be tempted to move them to a wire rack too quickly). Serve with a mandatory cup of tea.

Coconut Rose Ladoos

SERVES 6

150g desiccated coconut

260g condensed milk

1 teaspoon butter

2 tablespoons Turkish rose petal jam

¼ teaspoon ground cardamom

Drop of pink food colouring

To Decorate

2 tablespoons freeze-dried strawberry powder

2 tablespoons desiccated coconut

2 tablespoons pistachios, toasted and chopped

The ladoo is a south-east Asian sweet that is shaped into little spheres and served at religious or festive occasions. These coconut rose ones are exceptionally moist and moreish and make the perfect homemade edible gift, as they are quick and easy to make and look wonderful.

Put the desiccated coconut, condensed milk and butter into a non-stick pan and stir together. Place over a medium heat and cook, stirring occasionally, for 4–5 minutes, making sure that the coconut does not catch at any point. The mixture will be ready when it looks like a thick, slightly sticky mix that is coming away from the edge of the pan.

Add the rose petal jam and ground cardamom and stir vigorously to combine (it will stiffen up slightly as it cools).

Transfer half the ladoo mixture to a bowl. Add a drop of pink food colouring to the mixture left in the pan and stir well to give a lovely bright pink hue. Decant this pink coconut ladoo mixture into another bowl and set aside to cool. Once the ladoo mixture is cool enough to handle, use lightly oiled hands to shape it into small bite-sized balls (see Note).

Now comes the exciting part: roll the white and pink coconut balls into either the freeze-dried strawberry powder, desiccated coconut or toasted pistachios to create a selection of different coloured sweets.

Store in an airtight container for up to a week.

 NB *If when you come to rolling the mixture into balls you feel the mix is too wet, simply add a little extra desiccated coconut to firm the whole mixture up. If you find the mixture is too dry, add a tablespoon of milk or melted butter to soften.*

Masala Chai Crème Caramel

with Salted Dates

SERVES 4–6

550ml whole milk

5 cardamom pods, bruised

4 cloves

1 cinnamon stick

Small thumb-sized piece of fresh
ginger

3 Assam tea bags

2 eggs

3 egg yolks

3 tablespoons honey

110g sugar

110ml water

To Decorate

250g Medjool dates, finely
chopped

Sea salt

The geography of the Mughal Empire was crucial to its
development. The fertile landscape was perfect for agriculture
and the production of tea. In 1612 the British East India Company
won trading concessions from the Mughal emperors. Thus, with
the approval of local Indian rulers, the worldwide import of tea
commenced.

This dessert is a celebration of masala chai, the staple sweet spiced
tea of India and Pakistan. I fondly remember a family trip to India,
drinking masala tea in a small tavern overlooking the Taj Mahal, a
Mughal monument built by the Mughal Emperor Shah Jahan. In
this recipe, the tea-flavoured custard should be just set, soft and
glossy with dark sweet caramel dripping onto the plate.

Put the milk, cardamom pods, cloves, cinnamon, ginger and tea bags
into a pan and allow to infuse over a low heat for 15–20 minutes.
Strain the warm milk, discarding the tea bags, ginger, cinnamon, cloves
and cardamom pods and set aside.

Put the eggs and egg yolks into a bowl with the honey and stir gently
until combined. Pour over the warm milk mixture and whisk gently,
making sure that the mixture does not froth. Strain and pour into a jug.

Put the sugar and measured water into a small pan, place over a low
heat to dissolve the sugar, then boil rapidly without stirring, until it is
a rich dark brown colour. Immediately pour the caramel into a 15cm
soufflé dish or cake tin and swirl gently to coat the caramel evenly over
the bottom and sides. (Alternatively, pour the syrup into four to six
individual ramekins.) Allow to cool and set.

Preheat the oven to 160°C (140°C fan), gas mark 3.

Pour the tea-flavoured custard over the caramel and place the dish or dishes in a deep roasting tray. Pour in enough warm water to come halfway up the sides of the dish (this is known as bain-marie). Cover with foil and bake for 1–1½ hours (45 minutes if you are making in individual ramekins), or until the custard has just set. Carefully lift out of the bain-marie and allow to cool and chill completely in the fridge. When you are ready to serve, pass a sharp knife around the edge of the custard and invert onto a serving plate. The liquid caramel will pour out over the set glossy custard. Decorate with finely chopped dates and a sprinkle of sea salt before serving.

Betel Leaf Mouth Freshener

SERVES 10

3 betel leaves, thinly sliced (look online or in Asian supermarkets)

180g gulkand (coarse rose petal jam – see Note)

30g desiccated coconut, plus extra for coating

2 tablespoons fennel seeds, crushed

½ teaspoon ground cardamom

60g sultanas

4 tablespoons maple syrup

Few drops of red food colouring

30g blanched almonds, finely chopped

The tradition of eating betel leaf after a heavy meal is centuries old. The famous fifteenth-century cookbook *Ni'matnama*, or *Book of Delights*, even has an important section devoted solely to the preparation of betel leaves. Betel leaf mouth freshener is also known as *paan* today. Empress Noor Jehan, wife of Emperor Jahangir is said to have made it popular among women of the time. It was thought to aid digestion after a heavy meal, freshen the mouth and give an attractive pink hue to the lips.

_____

Put all the ingredients, except the chopped almonds, into a food processor or blender and blitz for 30–45 seconds, or until the mixture starts coming together and all the ingredients are well combined.

Tip the mixture into a bowl and add the chopped almonds. At this point you can adjust the consistency of the mix. If it appears too soft add a little more desiccated coconut until it has a firmer consistency. Shape the paan into small grape-sized balls and roll each ball in desiccated coconut before serving. They will keep for a few weeks in an airtight container.

 NB *Gulkand, or gulqand, is a south-east Asian sweet preserve made of rose petals and jaggery or cane sugar. Gul means 'flower' in Persian and Urdu, and qand is the Arabic term for 'sweet'. It is quite different from the Turkish-style rose petal jams, which are much runnier in texture.*

Drinks

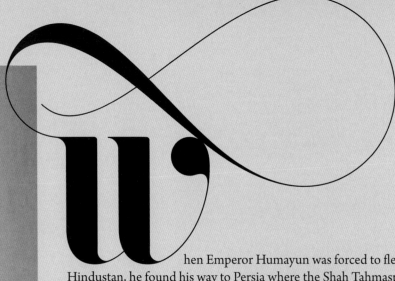

When Emperor Humayun was forced to flee Hindustan, he found his way to Persia where the Shah Tahmasp of Persia offered him shelter. A magnificent feast was held to mark Emperor Humayun's reception, emphasising the grandeur and prestige of the refugee emperor.

The courtly hospitality of the Persians was outstanding. The Shah of Persia commanded his men to serve Emperor Humayun 'in the manner that one would serve one's own King'. 'Let arrangement be made day by day for sweet and pleasant drinks,' proclaimed the King. 'When he in his glory and fortune shall direct a halt, let rose water sherbet and wholesome lemon juice be prepared and poured out, after having been cooled with snow and ice'.

Refreshing sweet and savoury yoghurt-based drinks called lassis and ice-cold sherbets are a staple in the Indian subcontinent today. They hydrate and revitalise millions in the searing summer heat. Nowadays, ice is readily available, but in the Mughal era it was transported from remote north Indian mountain peaks to palace kitchens in bustling metropolitan cities, where it was used to hydrate the emperors on scorching summer nights.

Tea became popular in the latter part of the Mughal dynasty with the emergence of the British Empire. However, historical accounts by author Edward Terry point to coffee being the preferred hot beverage in the era of Emperor Jahangir. During Mughal times, the Chandni Chowk region of Delhi was home to numerous coffee houses; popular gathering spots for men to drink hot coffee, smoke hookahs, listen to poetry and discuss politics.

Lemon & Rose Sherbet

SERVES 4

300ml water
6 tablespoons demerara sugar
5 tablespoons rose water
80ml lemon juice
Pink food colouring (optional)
8–12 ice cubes
100g lemon sorbet
Chilled sparkling water, to top up
Fresh rose petals, to decorate

Put the measured water and demerara sugar into a pan and place over a high heat. Stir well to dissolve the sugar and bring the mixture to the boil, then lower the heat and simmer until the mixture has reduced down to the consistency of a sticky syrup, such as honey or maple syrup. Be careful to not let the sugar syrup caramelise and try not to stir too often as this may cause the sugar to crystallise. Allow the sugar syrup to cool and then add the rose water, lemon juice and a few drops of pink food colouring, if liked.

Pour the cooled lemon and rose syrup equally into four tall glasses. Add a few ice cubes and a scoop of lemon sorbet to each glass. Top up each glass with cold sparkling water, decorate with a few fresh rose petals, as pictured opposite, and serve immediately.

'Angoor' Grape & Ginger Sherbet

SERVES 4

500ml water
1 cinnamon stick
4 tablespoons tamarind pulp
500g purple grapes, (ideally Muscat)
2 heaped teaspoons grated ginger
½ teaspoon black salt (or use sea salt)
8–12 ice cubes
Handful of fresh mint leaves

Put the measured water, cinnamon stick and tamarind pulp into a pan and bring to the boil. Add the grapes and ginger to the boiling water and then take the pan off the heat. Leave the mixture to cool.

When cool, remove and discard the cinnamon stick, pour the mixture into a blender and blitz for about a minute to release the juice from the grapes. Strain the mixture through a muslin cloth into a large bowl and add the black salt.

Ladle the grape and ginger sherbet into glasses filled with ice cubes. Serve immediately, decorated with mint leaves.

Papaya & Honey Lassi

300g ripe papaya fruit, peeled and deseeded

4 tablespoons honey

¼ teaspoon ground cardamom

250ml buttermilk

150ml natural yoghurt

8 ice cubes

Handful of toasted pistachios, to decorate

Pour all the ingredients except the pistachios into a blender and blitz to a smooth, salmon-pink-coloured purée.

Crush the pistachios in a pestle and mortar to form a nutty rubble. Pour the papaya and honey lassi into tall glasses and scatter the toasted pistachios over the top, as pictured opposite. Serve immediately.

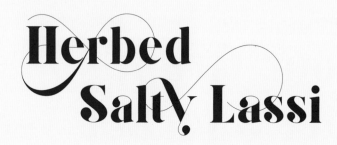

Herbed Salty Lassi

1 teaspoon grated ginger

1 heaped teaspoon cumin seeds, dry-roasted

500ml natural yoghurt

8 ice cubes

½ teaspoon black salt (optional)

Handful of fresh mint leaves

Handful of fresh coriander, roughly chopped

Put the ginger, cumin seeds, natural yoghurt, ice cubes and salt into a blender and blitz for about 1 minute. Taste at this stage and add more salt if desired.

Add the mint and coriander to the blender and briefly blitz again – the idea is to break the herbs down into small pieces, not to create a drink that is a homogenous shade of green, so small flecks of herb should be visible. Serve as a cooling accompaniment to any rich or spicy meal.

Mango, Date & Fennel Lassi

SERVES 4

6 Medjool dates

120ml tinned Alphonso mango pulp

1 heaped teaspoon fennel seeds

300ml buttermilk

200ml natural yoghurt

6 ice cubes

4 tablespoons good-quality date syrup, such as Basra (optional)

Put the dates into a blender together with the mango pulp, fennel seeds, buttermilk, natural yoghurt and ice cubes and blitz to a smooth purée. Strain the lassi through a sieve to remove any large pieces of date skin or fennel seeds that have escaped blending.

Spoon the date syrup, if using, around the edges of the serving glasses. Gently pour in the mango lassi and serve.

Saffron Iced Green Tea

SERVES 4

2 good-quality green tea bags

Good pinch of premium-quality saffron threads

5 cardamom pods, lightly bruised

1 tablespoon fennel seeds, lightly crushed

1 litre boiling water

100g icing sugar

8–12 ice cubes

1 lemon, very thinly sliced

Put the green tea bags, saffron threads, cardamom pods and fennel seeds into a large jug and pour over the measured boiling water. Leave the tea bags and spices to steep and infuse the water as it cools.

When the green tea reaches room temperature, strain it into a clean jug, discarding the tea bags, cardamom pods and fennel seeds. Add the icing sugar, ice cubes and lemon slices and stir well to dissolve the icing sugar. Taste your iced tea – I prefer to keep it a little less sugary, but you may wish to increase the quantity of icing sugar or lemon juice to your taste.

Serve on a hot summer day.

 NB For a little something extra, add a teaspoon of basil seeds to the bottom of each glass before pouring in the tea. Stir well and leave for about 5 minutes to give the basil seeds time to rehydrate.

Masala Chai

SERVES 4

1.5 litres water
1 cinnamon stick
6 green cardamom pods
6 cloves
Thumb-sized piece of fresh ginger, peeled and thinly sliced
1 tablespoon fennel seeds
50g demerara sugar
2 tablespoons loose Assam tea
100–200ml evaporated milk

Pour the measured water into a pan and add the cinnamon stick, cardamom pods, cloves, ginger, fennel seeds and demerara sugar. Bring to the boil; once the mixture has reached boiling point and all the sugar has dissolved, add the loose tea. Lower the heat and simmer for a further 20–25 minutes, allowing the tea leaves to release their full flavour.

Add the evaporated milk to the pan, depending on how milky you like your tea. Simmer for a further 2–3 minutes before passing the tea through a strainer into a teapot. For authenticity, serve the masala chai in glass teacups, as pictured opposite.

Rose Latte

SERVES 1

1 double espresso, cooled
1 tablespoon rose water
2 tablespoons demerara sugar
2 teaspoon dried rose petals
250ml semi-skimmed milk
Dollop of whipped cream

Pour the double espresso and rose water into the bottom of a cup.

Blitz the demerara sugar and dried rose petals in a spice or coffee grinder (or use a pestle and mortar) to form a rose-sugar dust.

Heat the milk in a small pan until it just comes up to the boil. Remove from the heat and slowly pour the milk over the coffee and rose water. Top the latte with whipped cream and a sprinkling of the rose-sugar dust. Serve immediately.

Index

Picture Credits & Captions

2/saiko3p/Shutterstock: A floral design of precious stones on marble from the walls of the Taj Mahal in Agra, India.

8/courtesy of Saliha Mahmood Ahmed: A picture of Saliha's nano (maternal grandmother) Asma Noor Elahi, aged 17 years.

11/Niday Picture Library/Alamy: An historical map of India during the Mughal era, coloured by province. Illustrated circa 1728 by German mapmaker Georg Matthäus Seutter.

13/robertharding/Alamy: The Taj Mahal at dawn, in Agra, India.

22–23, 62–63, 92–93, 128–129, 148–149, 176–177, 200–201, 222–223/Fat Jackey/Shutterstock: A Mughal wall painting at the City Palace in Jaipur, India.

38/Zvonimir Atletic/Shutterstock: A wall painting in the Chandra Mahal, City Palace in Jaipur, India.

58–59/saiko3p/Shutterstock: A beautiful pattern from the walls of the City Palace in Jaipur, India.

77/Everett Collection Historical/Alamy: An Indian Mughal watercolour painting of the Emperor Shah Jahan watching an elephant fight, by Bulaqi in 1639.

86–87/Mikadun/Shutterstock: A beautiful pattern from the walls of the Amber Fort in Jaipur, India.

107/The Picture Art Collection/Alamy: An illustration from the Baburnama, the memoir of Emperor Babur, founder of the Mughal empire.

108/saiko3p/Shutterstock: A beautiful pattern on a courtyard wall at the City Palace in Udaipur, India.

116/Zvonimir Atletic/Shutterstock: A wall painting in the Chandra Mahal, City Palace in Jaipur, India.

125/Dinodia Photos/Alamy: A miniature painting on ivory of Emperor Shah Jahan.

136/Heritage Image Partnership Ltd/Alamy: A Mughal painting of flowers on silk, originating from India in the 17th century.

137/Kristin Perers: Yellow chiffon fabric with a floral design hand-stitched by Saliha's maternal grandmother Asma Noor Elahi.

139/robertharding/Alamy: A beautiful Mughal fresco from the walls of the Juna Mahal in Dungarpur, India.

144–145/saiko3p/Shutterstock: Mughal arches inside the Red Fort of Agra, India.

156/saiko3p/Shutterstock: A beautiful pattern from the walls of the City Palace in Jaipur, India.

166/Phuong D. Nguyen/Shutterstock: A floral design of precious stones on marble from the walls of the Taj Mahal in Agra, India.

182/Mikadun/Shutterstock: A Mughal wall painting at the Nahargarh Fort in Jaipur, India.

185/The Picture Art Collection/Alamy: An illustration from the Baburnama, the memoir of Emperor Babur, founder of the Mughal empire.

224/Kristin Perers: A photograph of betel leaves, which for centuries were eaten at the end of a meal. They were thought to aid digestion and freshen the mouth. See page 259 for the Betel Leaf Mouth Freshener.

261/saiko3p/Shutterstock: A beautiful pattern from the walls of the City Palace in Jaipur, India.

Acknowledgements

First and foremost, I would like to acknowledge my husband **Usman Ahmed**, whose companionship and friendship are a driving force in my life.

A huge thank you to my parents and parents-in-law for their constant support and undying faith in my culinary abilities. A particular thanks to my mother-in-law, **Rukhsana Ahmed**, for always offering assistance when recipe testing and my mama, **Amina Mahmood**, for making the Mughal vision a reality for everyone.

Thank you to my colleagues in the **NHS** who have always given me the flexibility and support to pursue my food-writing career.

Thanks to **John Torode** and **Gregg Wallace** for being fantastic mentors and making me believe in my style of cookery, and to the whole *MasterChef* team for giving me the most amazing opportunity a home cook could ask for.

I would like to express my deepest gratitude to **Heather Holden-Brown** and **Cara Armstrong** at HHB Agency who have so gracefully navigated me through this creative process and remain my mentors, confidantes and close friends.

The creation of *Khazana* was, of course, a team effort. Thank you to **Nicky Ross** and **Natalie Bradley** at Hodder & Stoughton for leading and creating this team, having faith in my ability to write and for loving the food of the Mughals as much as I do.

There are a number of creative geniuses in our midst! **Kristin Perers**, the most incredible food photographer; **Ellie Mulligan**, an exceedingly talented food stylist; and **Louie Waller**, prop stylist extraordinaire. The amazing photographs in this book are a testament to the magnificent work of these powerhouses. I must also mention **Toni Musgrave** who worked relentlessly in the studio kitchen despite being heavily pregnant.

A special thank you to **Nikki Dupin** and her entire team for immersing themselves so wholeheartedly into the artwork of the Mughals and for creating visuals that are not only memorable today, but I am certain will stand the test of time. I could not have asked for anything more. Thanks, also, to **Clare Sayer** for her fantastic job copy-editing the text.

Additionally, a huge thank you to **Sarah Christie**, **Claudette Morris**, **Rebecca Mundy**, **Caitriona Horne** and everyone at Hodder & Stoughton for their tireless efforts in getting *Khazana* from just a manuscript to the shelf and through to the reader.

Lastly, I have to mention two influential people who have instilled the love for literature in me from a young age. My late grandfather, **Salahuddin Mahmood**, who would have been so proud to see *Khazana*. And my daddy, **Tariq Mahmood**, who knows how special he is to everyone.

First published in Great Britain in 2018
by Hodder & Stoughton
An Hachette UK company

1

Copyright © Saliha Mahmood Ahmed 2018
Photography by Kristin Perers © Hodder & Stoughton 2018

See page 283 for additional picture credits.

The following recipes first appeared in 2017 on BBC's
MasterChef, produced by Shine TV in association with Ziji
productions: Lamb Shanks in Pomegranate & Date Syrup with
Aubergine & Chickpea Couscous (see page 70); Rose-scented
Chicken & Rose Shorba with Saffron Rice (see page 102); Sea
Bream Pakoras with Brown Sauce & Spicy Chips (see page
130); Swordfish Steaks with Tomato, Ginger & Fenugreek
Sauce (see page 142); Jewelled Persian Rice (see page 180);
Cashew Dum Biryani with Potato & White Poppy Seeds (see
page 190); Coriander, Cashew & Golden Sultana Dip (see
page 213); Smoky Eastern Ketchup (see page 220); Buttermilk,
Saffron & Orange Blossom Panna Cotta with Candied
Pistachios (see page 240).

A CIP catalogue record for this title is available from the British
Library

Hardback ISBN 978 1 473 67856 9
eBook ISBN 978 1 473 67857 6

Editorial Director: Nicky Ross
Project Editor: Natalie Bradley
Copy-editor: Clare Sayer
Design and art direction: nic&lou
Photographer: Kristin Perers
Food Stylist: Ellie Mulligan
Props Stylist: Louie Waller
Production Manager: Claudette Morris

Colour origination by Altaimage
Printed and bound in Italy by LEGO SpA

Hodder & Stoughton policy is to use papers that are natural,
renewable and recyclable products and made from wood grown
in sustainable forests. The logging and manufacturing processes
are expected to conform to the environmental regulations of the
country of origin.

Hodder & Stoughton Ltd
Carmelite House
50 Victoria Embankment
London EC4Y 0DZ

www.hodder.co.uk